Praise for Betty Fussell's

My Kitchen Wars

"A wonderful, humorous book."   —Alice Waters

"A tart, elegant memoir in which food is battle, power, marriage, sex, love, literature and philosophy . . . *My Kitchen Wars* is a multilayered, luscious book that readers will want to taste and savor for its many pleasures again and again."
                    —Denise Gess, *The Atlanta Journal-Constitution*

"Entertaining . . . with delicious, gossipy tidbits about famous people, such as Philip Roth and Kingsley Amis . . . compelling because of its expansiveness, both in the scope of history that it covers, and in its emotional sincerity."
                    —Susan Dundon, *The Philadelphia Inquirer*

"Fussell serves up the story of her life with the same cutting wit and pungent detail that distinguishes her cookbooks."
                    —Wendy Smith, *Elle*

"A clever, seductive, funny, tightly composed meditation that really does make palpable the complicated mess of memory through the metaphor of cooking—sensual, brutal, artful, manipulative."   —Patricia Unterman, *San Francisco Examiner*

Also by Betty Fussell

Mabel: Hollywood's First I-Don't-Care Girl

Masters of American Cookery

I Hear America Cooking

Eating In

Food in Good Season

Home Plates

The Story of Corn

Crazy for Corn

Home Bistro

My Kitchen Wars

My Kitchen Wars

Betty Fussell

North Point Press

Farrar, Straus and Giroux

New York

North Point Press
A division of Farrar, Straus and Giroux
19 Union Square West, New York 10003

Copyright © 1999 by Betty Fussell
All rights reserved
Distributed in Canada by Douglas & McIntyre Ltd.
Printed in the United States of America
Designed by Jonathan D. Lippincott
First published in 1999 by North Point Press
First paperback edition, 2000

Library of Congress Cataloging-in-Publication Data
Fussell, Betty Harper.
    My kitchen wars / Betty Fussell.
        p.   cm.
    ISBN 0-86547-603-9 (pbk.)
    1. Fussell, Betty Harper. 2. Gourmets—United States Biography.
I. Title.
TX649.F87F87   1999
641.3'092—dc21   99–25954

The names of some individuals, along with identifying details, have been
changed to protect their privacy.

Acknowledgments

This work exceeded its estimated cooking time by so many hours of so many years that I am more than usually grateful to those who freed me from kitchen work so that I could write about it. For that freedom I thank the MacDowell Colony for appointing me a DeWitt Wallace/Reader's Digest Fellow, the Corporation of Yaddo, the Djerassi Resident Artists Program, the Millay Colony for the Arts, the Villa Montalvo Artist Residency Program, and the Hawthornden Castle International Retreat for Writers. My editor, Becky Saletan, knows just how much I owe her, and I thank her for not telling.

To my companions in arms
Pat, Glenna, Georgine, Sandy

Contents

"Memory is hunger."

—Ernest Hemingway

"Ike runs the country and I turn the lamb chops."

—Mamie Eisenhower

My Kitchen Wars

Assault and Battery

COME IN, COME IN. I've just made coffee and it smells, as good coffee should, of bitter chocolate.

Don't mind the mess. It's always this way, because a kitchen is in the middle of things, in the middle of life, as I'm living it now, this moment, the detritus of the past heaped like a midden everywhere you look. That squat brown bean pot we got in 1949 for our first kitchen, in a Boston slum, when I didn't know beans about cooking. That tarnished copper bowl I bought at Dehillerin in Paris in 1960, used heavily for soufflés during my Julia decade, which I haven't used since for anything at all.

I like food because it's in the middle of the mess. I like thinking about what I ate yesterday, what I'll eat tonight, what we're eating now—this hot crumbly shortbread full of butter and toasted pecans. So delicious. So tangible, sensuous, real. I can hold it in my hand, in my mouth, on my tongue. I can turn it over in my mind. I can count on it. The next bite will bring the same intense pleasure the last bite did, and the same pleasure tomorrow, if there are any bites left.

Do you take milk, and would you like it frothed? This little
glass jar has a plunger fitted with a wire-mesh screen, and when
I pump it up and down, the hot milk thickens into a blanket of
foam. It's the little things that count, and everything in my
kitchen counts heavily. Look at this olive pitter that I use
maybe twice a year, this shrimp deveiner which removes that
telltale line of gut in a trice, this avocado skinner, ingeniously
fiddle-shaped to allow me to separate soft flesh from shell in a
single motion. When I try to explain to my grown children, to
friends, to myself, why I still live a kitchen life, I begin with the
naming of kitchen parts. Well-made implements, well chosen
and well used, turn labor into art, routine into joy.

And yet the French got it right when they christened the
kitchen arsenal the *batterie de cuisine*. Hunger, like lust in action, is savage, extreme, rude, cruel. To satisfy it is to do battle,
deploying a full range of artillery—crushers, scrapers, beaters,
roasters, gougers, grinders, to name but a few of the thousand
and two implements that line my walls and cram my drawers—
in the daily struggle to turn ingredients into edibles for devouring mouths. Life eats life, and if we are to live, others must
die—just as if we are to love, we must die a little ourselves.

I've spent most of my life doing kitchen battle, feeding others and myself, torn between the desire to escape and the impulse to entrench myself further. When social revolutions
hustled women out of the kitchen and into the boardroom, I
seemed to be caught *in flagrante*, with a pot holder in my hand.
I knew that the position of women like myself was of strategic
importance in the war between the sexes. But if you could
stand the heat, did you have to get out of the kitchen? For even
as I chafed at kitchen confinement, cooking had begun its long

conquest of me. Food had infiltrated my heart, seduced my brain, and ravished my senses. Peeling the layers of an onion, spooning out the marrow of a beef bone, laying bare the skeleton of a salmon were acts very like the act of sex, ecstatically fusing body and mind.

While cooking is a brutal business, in which knives cut, whisks whip, forks prick, mortars mash, and stoves burn, still it is our most civilized act. Within its cardinal points—pots, a fan, a sink, a stove—my kitchen encompasses earth, air, water, and fire. These are the elements of nature that cooking transforms to make the raw materials of food, and the murderous acts of cooking and eating it, human. Cooking connects every hearth fire to the sun and smokes out whatever gods there be—along with the ghosts of all our kitchens past, and all the people who have fed us with love and hate and fear and comfort, and whom we in turn have fed. A kitchen condenses the universe.

Food, far more than sex, is the great leveler. Just as every king, prophet, warrior, and saint has a mother, so every Napoleon, every Einstein, every Jesus has to eat. Eating is an in-body experience, a lowest common denominator, by nature funny, like the banana peel or the pie-in-the-face of slapstick. The subversive comedy of food is incremental. Little laughs add up to big ones, big enough to poke a hole in our delusions of star-wars domination and bring us down to earth. The gut, like the bum, makes the whole world one.

That's why I write about food. It keeps me grounded in small pleasures that add up to big ones, that kill time by savoring it, in memory and anticipation. Food conjugates my past and future and keeps me centered in the present, in my body, my animal self. It keeps my gut and brain connected to each other as well as to the realities of the world outside, to all those other forms of being—animal, vegetable, mineral—of which I am a part. Food keeps me humble and reminds me that I'm as kin to a cabbage or a clam as to a Bengal tiger on the prowl.

That's why I decline the epic view from the battlements in favor of the view from my kitchen window, fogged by steam from the soup in the pot. When I chop onions and carrots, crush garlic, and hunt out meaty bones for my soup, I'm doing what I've done for decades and what women before me have done from the beginning of time, when they used stones instead of knives and ashes instead of pots. There's comfort in this, in the need, in the craft, in the communion of hands and of hungers. A wooden spoon links me to my grandmother in her apron and to the woman who taught Jacob to stir a mess of pottage. History can turn on a spoon, on a soup.

And so of arms and the woman I sing, while we drink our coffee, you and I. The singer is an "old stove," as they say in San Francisco of a woman who's done time at the burners. But the songs of an old stove, no matter how darkly they glitter, are gay.

To Arms with
Squeezer and Slicer

MY DAD'S FAVORITE KITCHEN IMPLEMENT was the orange squeezer, not the elemental hand squeezer with a serrated cone on which you place half an orange and, pressing hard, turn the orange clockwise, releasing pulp into the container below. His was a 1930s improvement made of dull metal alloy. He put the orange half into a container elevated on a stand, and when he brought the handle down, as if pumping water, a thick metal square squeezed the orange flat so that its juice squirted through an opening. He'd had lots of experience with pump handles, and a pump that squirted orange juice instead of water was better than the Well of Cana that turned water into wine.

Dad loved to squeeze oranges. He never squeezed people or even touched them. Bodies embarrassed him. But oranges he could hold in his hand with impunity. Oranges he loved. That's why we lived in California, and that's how it happened that I was born and my mother died in a kitchen in the middle of an orange grove. California was the romance of my dad's life, and he never got over it.

The pull of the West had long ago drawn my Lowland Scots ancestors, first across the Irish Sea to County Derry and Tyrone, then across the Atlantic Ocean to Pennsylvania, down the Appalachians to Virginia and on to Ohio and Illinois, beyond the Missouri to Colorado, and finally over the Rockies, stopping only when further west meant east. By the late nineteenth century they moved to the galloping rhythm of a St. Andrews Society versifier who'd somehow got stuck in Philadelphia:

> To the West, to the West, to the land of the free,
> Where the mighty Missouri rolls down to the sea;
> Where a man is a man even though he must toil,
> And the poorest may gather the fruits of the soil.

They would have been appalled to learn that their descendants were called Scotch-Irish, as if a single one of them would have mingled blood with Papists when they paused in Ireland on their long roll west.

Of all the Scots in the list of begats pasted into our family Bible, the Erskines were the fiercest. Their Calvinism was a straight shot of Knox, with no mediating chaser. My father's mother, Carrie Hadassah Erskine, was a descendant of Presbyterian Dissenters unto the ninth and tenth generations, including the Reverend Ebenezer Erskine of Stirling, who in 1743 preached his most famous sermon, "Christ considered as the Nail fastened to a sure Place, bearing all the Glory of his Father's House." The carpentry metaphor was apt for a people compelled to keep moving their Father's House from place to place, the better to hammer in Christ the Nail.

If the housing wars of the eighteenth century pitched Christ against Satan, Protestant against Catholic, Calvin against the Pope, the street fights were Presbyters against one another, each lit by the lamp of God. The moment one Scottish gang split from the main division, another rose to fight it. New Licht Burghers battled Old Licht Burghers until both were attacked by New and Old Licht Anti-Burghers. Such were the wars before the truce of the United Secession Church in 1820 produced the oxymoronic United Presbyterians of America.

This was the Church and this the stock that spawned a long line of farming ministers and doctors before my father's father, Charles Sumner Harper, dissented from the traditional medicine practiced by his father and left the family farm in Kansas to study osteopathy in Des Moines. From there he moved on west to Greeley, Colorado, for the sake of his wife's health. In a family photo, I see Grandpa H. in his office, a big comfortable man who sits in a wooden rocking chair behind a desk that is bare but for its proud trophy, a telephone. In the companion photo, his wife sits small and erect, with a grin as wide as her sidesaddle, atop her favorite gray workhorse, Minnie, on their nearby farm.

My dad, Josias Meryl Harper, was thirty years old and president of the student body at Colorado State Teachers College in Greeley in 1922 when he met the organist, a music professor five years his senior named Ruby Hazel Kennedy. Six feet tall, with a bony face, Roman nose, dimpled chin, and ready smile, Meryl was an attractive man, a hard worker, and as upright as a fence post. His handsome younger brother, Roy, had graduated the year before, but Dad's studies had been delayed by military service. Roy would go on to find Eden in Brazil, as a Presbyterian missionary, but my father had already found it in California. As a naval recruit during World War I, he had been sent to San Francisco Bay to Goat Island, renamed Treasure, and had spent the war in a hospital bed on Mare Island after abdominal surgery for adhesions went awry. Following a medical discharge and a second bout of surgery, he spent the next two years recuperating on his parents' farm and vowing to get back to California. In his senior year he married the music professor and at graduation moved to paradise, as he'd vowed, with his bride and their month-old baby boy.

A photo of my mother in the college catalogue shows a round-cheeked woman with a gentle face and smile, thin-rimmed spectacles covering her brown eyes, and a puff of wavy hair that I'm told was auburn as autumn leaves when she was young. Miss Hazel Kennedy, the catalogue explains, laid the foundation for her successful career with a course at the University School of Music in Lincoln, Nebraska, before studying at the National Academy of Music at Carnegie Hall in New York City. She was the only one of my predecessors to reverse direction and go east.

Like the Harpers and Erskines on my father's side, the Kennedys and Culvers had moved in prairie schooners unremittingly east to west, fighting Indians along the way. My mother's mother, Ellen Josephine Culver, had the writing itch, and in 1928 she wrote her "Memories of Early Days," scribbling with a pencil on both sides and in the margins of what are now tattered sheets. From these, I know that her mother, Hannah Carpenter, pushed west from Ohio to the Iowa frontier with the family of a married sister in 1840, when Hannah was seventeen. I know that Hannah got married in her uncle's log house in a snowstorm three years later, and that she doffed her lace cap with its yards of white satin ribbon to put on flannel and linsey in time to do the chores when they got back to their newlyweds cabin down the Magnolia River. I know that one Sunday after a hard thunderstorm, the couple went for a walk in

the sun and killed thirty rattlers before they got home. I know
that on a day when the men were cutting grain in one field
while the women shocked it in another, the women saw a large
group of Indians crossing their field and hid all night in a grain
shock because they were afraid the Indians would return to
burn the house.

Grandma Kennedy's father died of typhoid before she was
born, but she was told that he'd asked his family to sing "I'm
Going Home to Die No More" on the day he passed into the
Beyond. As a girl, Grandma K. remembered, she saw off her
cousin Cummings and his brothers as they went to answer their
country's call to arms during the Civil War. As the train pulled
away, she cried, "Cummings, come back," but Cummings did
not, for he too died of typhoid while guarding rebel soldiers in
Illinois. The women of her house cut up linen to make lint for
wounded soldiers while the kids played soldiers by killing rebel
mice in the granary with bow and arrow. Ellen was so quick
with her hands that she caught mice by the tail and hung on to
them even though they bit her fingers until blood dripped.
"Lew said that if I let them go, I was not a good soldier," she
recalled. "Such was the spirit drilled even into babies."

She married Parks Ira Kennedy in 1880 and homesteaded in
the territory of Nebraska. Parks was a well digger, but he was
also a builder and cabinetmaker. He dug the first well and built
the first church at one crossroads after another. He was a musical man who played the French horn as sweetly as he sang, and
once Christ the Nail was fixed in his Father's House, he organized the church choir while Ellen, who'd been trained in elo-
cution, set up the Sunday school. In a later age they might have
taken to the road as an evangelical duo, she the poet-preacher
and he the accompanying choirmaster, to declare war on the
wide world of Sin.

Grandma K. lived long enough to celebrate her sixty-sixth wedding anniversary as a passel of grandsons fought World War II. In her century she brought God and civilization to the prairies in the particular alliance of Calvinism with the genteel arts that characterized the homesteaders of her generation and created the powerful matriarchs of Victorian America. Her children remembered her as the head of an ever-expanding commune of one son and six daughters, two hired girls, at least one hired man, and an accumulation of foster boys whom she welcomed after they'd been sent packing at fourteen, according to Swedish farm traditions in America at that time, to make their own way in the new country.

On a sweltering July day in 1904, Grandma K. delivered, as president of the Nebraska branch of the Women's Christian Temperance Union, a Chautauqua lecture entitled "Some Evils Which Threaten Our Girls."

> Did you ever see a lovelier picture than that produced by Dame Nature, on a winter's morning when plain, hill and dell are covered with a mantle of snow, glittering with diamonds or shimmering with pearls, as the changing sunbeams flash their golden lights over that spotless landscape? Did it not make you think of the world arrayed as a Bride to meet the Bridegroom? It is a scene to remind us of the purity of maidenhood before the evils of this life have left their stains and shadows upon its snowy whiteness. Alas! How very soon the contamination begins.

She must have valued the manuscript, because it too came down to me, page after worm-eaten page, detailing the evils of alcohol, tobacco, the dance hall—"an open door to the brothel"—and sensational novels which "give the agents of Satan a chance to do missionary work for the lower regions."

A decade earlier, Grandma K. herself had been contaminated, by consumption, which gave her a certain cachet and, long after she recovered, allowed her to retreat to her bed when convenient. By the time the two youngest girls were born, her eldest were well trained to look after them, and they remained a close-knit clan. Hazel was the fourth girl, and the rebel among them, the tomboy who'd join the boys in swinging down from the hayloft on a rope. Hazel was the ambitious one, the adventurous one, who went by herself on the Union Pacific Railroad to New York, where she'd gotten a scholarship to study at Dr. Wilbert Webster White's Bible Teacher's Training College while furthering her piano study at Carnegie Hall. Hazel was the professional one, in a family of accomplished amateur musicians. Hazel was also the fragile one, who overburdened her strength and overloaded her circuits, suffering a back injury in New York which triggered a nervous breakdown and recuperation in a rest home in New Jersey before she was sent home to Nebraska.

There were further breakdowns, and further interruptions to her studies while she worked for money to continue, but Hazel finally achieved her goal of teaching piano when she joined the music faculty at Colorado State Teachers College. She rented a big two-story house in Greeley and brought her sister Charlotte to live with her, along with several other female students who needed room and board. She brought her parents, too, who'd been homesteading in tiny Briggsdale, Colorado. The Kennedys probably met the Harpers in the First Presbyterian Church of Greeley, but neither family would have predicted that they'd both end up in Southern California, a mere forty miles apart, bonded by a pair of grandchildren.

My Kennedy grandparents went west first, to live with their eldest daughter, Lyda, and her husband, Bert. Bert was a builder and carpenter like his father-in-law, and together they built in the wilds outside Glendale a solid stuccoed house that sits on the top of Nob Hill in Eagle Rock exactly as it did eighty years ago. My parents were living further north, in Palo Alto, where Dad hurried to get his teaching credential at Stanford. But when a second baby boy was born sickly and died, Hazel's delicate nervous system broke down again, and they moved south so that Hazel could be with her parents. My father landed a job at Polytechnic High School in Riverside, where he would teach botany and biology for the next fifty years.

In a house crowded with three families, it must have seemed a bright idea for my parents and grandparents to start a chicken ranch together on two and a half acres in Riverside, further east. In the winter of 1926, Grandpa K. threw up a one-room garage meant to be temporary living quarters until he could build a permanent house. But it didn't take long for the Great Chicken Enterprise to collapse. My grandparents, abandoning chickens, returned to the house on Nob Hill, while my parents and their little boy stayed on at the "ranch."

Still, having abandoned the fog of Northern California for the sunshine of the south, my father never looked back. He squeezed fresh orange juice every morning at 6:30 sharp, day in and day out, summer and winter, before morning prayers. In California the miracle of oranges, like the miracle of sunshine, was a tangible daily witness to God's forgiveness of Adam's sin, the sin that brought blizzards to Kansas, breakdowns to nervous systems, and adhesions to bowels. The conception of seedless oranges, strung like Christmas balls in dark green groves in the middle of December when the sun shone bright, made

Riverside the site of miracles for which my family took responsibility. Hadn't the rootstock of the navel orange been discovered in the jungles of Brazil by a Presbyterian missionary just like my Uncle Roy?

Until his death at ninety-one, my father rejoiced in Riverside as a miracle like unto the orange itself. For him the city was an oasis created from a desert wilderness by the magic of progress. In fact, it had been engineered at the turn of the century by a gang of water thieves, who laid the foundation not only for the orange industry but also for the heavier industries generated by World War II, which eventually turned the City of Oranges into Smog City, U.S.A. Like other facts, this was one my father with encrusted red-rimmed eyes denied to his dying day. "Just a little haze," he'd say of the sulphurous yellow blanket that smothered the town.

I wonder how he euphemized the gray layer of dust that covered the orange grove I grew up in, on the wrong side of Riverside, in a cluster of shanties hard by the cement plant that some scalawag realtor had named Rivino Orchards. And I wonder how he greeted the news in the fall of 1926 that his wife was once again pregnant, this time with me. When Hazel married, she'd been told she shouldn't try to bear children because of her bad back, not to mention her delicate psyche. The Harpers blamed Hazel for getting pregnant and the Kennedys blamed Dad, both sides of the family perennially short of funds but never of blame.

Grandma K. moved back in to look after her daughter. So did thirteen-year-old Leona, Lyda's eldest daughter. As Leona wrote long after, the place was "hot as Hades, bleak and desolate with grit and dust over everything from the nearby cement works which kept up a high-pitched 'peanut' whistle all day long." Even as a teenager, she said, this godforsaken place had her crawling up the walls. Grandma K. hung a blanket between the bed where she slept with Leona and the bed where Dad and Hazel slept with little Bobby. Another blanket separated the bed quarters from the cooking and eating quarters. Scots cottars would have said this divided the *ben* from the *but*—the *but* the open hearth that sent smoke through a hole in the roof, the *ben* the bed in a wooden enclosure, with a little door in front for getting in and out.

I was very nearly born in the *but* of this hovel, at least as Leona tells it. Nobody else would admit I got born at all, because the subject of birthing was taboo. "The things men do to women, even in marriage," Grandma K. told her children and grandchildren, "are vile, disgusting, filthy, and sinful." However necessary for the procreation of the race, birthing babies was as terrible as Adam and Eve's first discovery of shame.

Leona remembers that she woke one morning to hear whispers behind the blanket that shielded Hazel and Dad. Grandma K. was telling my mother to stop fussing and get in the car. Dad had cranked up the Model T and was waiting for her outside the kitchen door. Leona couldn't imagine what was wrong with Hazel, who was groaning horribly, but Grandma got her out the door and off Dad went. Grandma had just set out pancakes for breakfast when Dad returned, said "It's a girl," and asked for a bucket of water and some rags. Leona started out the door to see what was up, but Grandma slammed the door in her face and cried, "Mercy, child, don't you dare go out there." Leona had already seen that the back seat of the car was covered with blood, and she was frantic because no one would tell her what terrible thing had happened to her aunt.

A few days later, Hazel returned with a pink baby in her arms, and whether Dad had actually stopped the car to help deliver the baby or whether he just told Hazel to hang on after it slipped out was never clear. The baby was named Betty, a name favored by Nebraskans then and since, and Ellen, after Grandma K. The baby had blue eyes and straight blond hair, like her father, although when she grew up she was said to be the spitting image of her mother. After the first few weeks, when Hazel and the baby seemed to be doing well, Grandma K. and Leona went home to Eagle Rock.

It must have been a relief to be whittled down to a mere foursome in the garage, but at the same time the days must have been long and exhausting and lonely for a woman over forty who had devoted herself to the practice of music in an earlier life. There was an upright piano in one corner of the garage, but there could have been little time to play it. Just keeping a new baby, a scrappy boy of four, and a husband in clean and ironed clothes would have been a full-time job in so primitive a house.

On the day of her death I see her, my fantasy colored by my brother's memories, wandering over to the piano while Bobby and I, now almost six and not quite two, played with empty spools of thread on the kitchen floor. She might have started a Bach fugue or a Chopin prelude or something merrier, like Saint-Saëns's *Rapsodie d'Auvergne*, before slamming the lid of the piano shut. She was often distracted, or so they said, given to nibbling things absentmindedly as she went about the house.

Next to the sink was an open tin of rat poison. In her distraction, she might have dipped a finger in the tin and put it in her mouth without realizing what it was. She might have. What Bob remembers is her falling to the floor, her mouth foaming, calling out to him to run, run quick and get help. Our nearest neighbor was a good fifteen-minute run for a small boy, and when Bobby got back with the neighbor, the man said she was gone and found a blanket to cover her. I was playing on the floor as if nothing had happened, but Bobby cried, because she had counted on him to get help and he had failed.

When genealogy became Dad's obsession in his geriatric years, he made hundreds of photocopies of the family tree, as if that might somehow elaborate its sparse branches. His written account of my mother's death was typically terse. "Hazel became ill, entered the Community Hospital, and passed away." In conversation, I don't remember his ever mentioning her by name. Nor did Grandpa and Grandma Harper, who took on the burden of raising her two small children, first at their Colorado farm and then, when they sold the farm two years later, at Rivino Orchards. It seemed that everyone, whether they wanted to or not, ended up in California.

Because I was so small and doubtless trouble, Hazel's sister Edna and her family took care of me that first winter in their house in Sterling, Colorado. I remember nothing except icicles hanging from the eaves and dripping on my head in the sun, an exotic watersport for an orange-grove kid. And all I remember of the summer I spent in Gilchrist, reunited with my brother and Dad, was the farmhouse kitchen and its icebox, concealing like Pandora's box my first full sensual experience of the hidden pleasures of the flesh. Bob remembers the farm as the happiest time in his life, spent outdoors with the farm horse and the chickens and the cows and the dogs. But what I remember is toddling over to the icebox, where the door had been left ajar, and finding within its coolness a big thick cube as golden as an orange and as smooth and velvety as ice cream. I took it out and licked it. It got slippery in my hands, creamed my mouth, melted on my tongue, and ran down my throat. By the time they found me, I had consumed the whole pound of it. It was clear I was destined for a lifelong romance with butter that would rival my father's love affair with oranges.

Butter, chickens, eggs. These were the staples of Grandma H.'s kitchen, in California as in Colorado. Wherever we moved, we kept chickens, and our eggs were always fresh. Eggs were an excuse for a bowlful of butter. Grandma H. boiled eggs two ways, soft or hard, and she served them in a bowl, two at a time. If they were soft, you stirred them with your spoon into the butter to make a kind of soup. If they were hard, she would slice them in her Presto 4-Way egg slicer, an efficient guillotine, the eight thin wires strung across its hinged top dropping neatly into the slots in its molded bottom. With her Erskine sense of humor, she'd pretend to crack an egg on my head while actually cracking it on the table, shell it quickly, then slice it in perfect Platonic circles, all white at each end, with white rims diminishing around bigger and bigger yellow centers toward the middle. Circles were useful for potato salad, but I preferred dice to circles, so that I could mash the white and yellow into a large blob of softened butter with my fork to make mashed butter flecked with egg. To make dice, Grandma would turn the sliced egg sideways in the hollow and drop the wires again to slice the other way. So simple a mechanism, so profound an effect.

When I think of Grandma and Grandpa H. at Rivino Orchards, I am always sitting in one or other of their laps, eating something. Grandma would sit me in her aproned lap while she quartered an apple with a dull table knife, cut out the core, then scraped the raw crisp flesh with the back of the knife to make instant applesauce, which she fed me from the knife's tip. Grandpa, whom Bobby and I called Bunco, would sit me on his overalled knees, open a jar of homemade jelly, usually apple or grape, and feed it to me "raw," with a spoon. Once while I was sitting on Bunco's lap in the yard outside the garage, a wasp flew by and stung me on the eyelid. My wail was an expression not only of pain but of outrage at betrayal. In a perilous world, Bunco's lap was supposed to be a sure Place, like Christ the Nail.

There were advantages to being raised by Fundamentalists for whom the Bible was a guidebook to history, geography, astronomy, archaeology, and genealogy. Grandma H., like all the women in my family, had been a schoolteacher, and at her knee when I was three or four I learned to recite both the multiplication table and the names of all the books of the Bible. The fact that Leviticus came before Numbers and Zechariah followed Haggai had to me the same logic as the eights coming before the nines or the fours following the threes. I learned the alphabet in a similar syncretism: A is for Abraham, B is for Bethlehem, C is for Christ. I knew verses and Psalms by heart long before I could read, and the story of the boy Samuel waking at night—"Here am I, Lord, send me"—was more real to me than the story of Peter Rabbit, hiding from Mr. McGregor in a flowerpot.

The topography of the Bible, overlaid with Bunyan's *Pilgrim's Progress*, mapped my real town and its surroundings. The Valley of the Shadow of Death was a real place, beyond the Mohave Desert, named Death Valley. The Slough of Despond was a place to the south of the actual Chocolate Mountains beyond Hemet, the Salton Sea. The hill where Christ was crucified, Golgotha, was Riverside's Mount Rubidoux, which we climbed at dawn every Easter with hundreds of others to witness, at the foot of the Cross planted there by a hotel entrepreneur, the miraculous Resurrection of Our Savior. In Riverside we were saved, glory hallelujah, by the annual rusting and renewing of Christ the Nail.

These were my years of safety, secure in salvation. Jesus

loved me; Grandpa and Grandma and the Bible and my Sunday
school teachers and the minister at Calvary Presbyterian
Church all told me so. My missionary Uncle Roy, home on fur-
lough, baptized me himself. A scrapbook labeled "Betty's" in
Grandma H.'s handwriting shows that I was accepted into the
Church on Easter Sunday 1935 after I'd attended confirmation
classes, "On Confession of Faith, Having Been Baptized," and
having tasted my first sanctified cracker and grape juice at
Good Friday communion service. A poem pasted in the scrapbook told me just how safe I was.

> *God made the Dark for children*
> *And birdies in their nest.*
> *All in the Dark* He *watches*
> *And guards us while we rest.*

There were a few loose twigs in the nest, however, a few
rockabye babies in treetops that came tumbling down in the
wind. My pet rooster, for one. I have a snapshot of me, plump
as a piglet, pulling him in my little red Flyer wagon around the
dirt yard beneath the orange trees. Chicken Little, I called him,
because it was the only chicken name I knew. One summer, after Bobby and I had spent a couple of weeks visiting Aunt Lyda
and Uncle Bert, I returned to the yard and called for Chicken
Little, but no cock came. He had disappeared without a trace.
Only years later did my grandparents confess that they'd taken
advantage of my absence to put him in the Sunday pot. They
laughed when they told it, but old as I was, and I must have
been in my teens, I was shocked.

I was no less shocked at twenty when I learned that the
cause of my mother's death was not necessarily the "accidental
poisoning" my family had claimed. I'd never thought to ques-

tion it. For me, my mother had existed only in photographs, in heaps of snapshots jumbled together in cardboard shirt boxes. I studied them endlessly as if the images were real as the heaven where she'd gone to live in her Father's House and where, Grandma H. assured me when pressed, I would join her and live happily ever after.

One day after I'd graduated from college, I was at my typewriter in the dining room filling out a job application when I asked Dad for some insurance document the form required. On the document he gave me was a note that at Hazel's death her life insurance money had been denied because the cause of her death was "unresolved."

"What does *that* mean?" I asked. Dad blushed, as if I'd asked him where babies come from. He cleared his throat several times, a chronic habit that intensified when he was embarrassed. "Well, there was some question at the time about whether it was fully accidental, given her past history of health problems, but of course you know how insurance companies are."

It was a thunderbolt, as sulphurous as the day outside was bright and clear. Was that the shame that had kept her name unspoken, her memory erased? Was that why the Kennedys never spoke of my father without an edge? She had killed herself, my saintly mother, looking down on me from heaven, the one sure Place. That was how she ended her kitchen wars. They must have been beyond bearing to leave behind a baby girl and a little boy who needed her then, and all their lives. I sensed a despair I tried to imagine but could not, except in bits and pieces, refracted in the constant anxiety of my father and grandparents over the state of my health. "You're such a nervous child," they'd say reprovingly, "just like your mother,"

warning me every time I jiggled my foot against succumbing to
St. Vitus' dance.

Not until twenty more years had passed did I come upon
anything to illuminate her despair. Grandma H. had kept a letter of Hazel's until she herself died, at eighty-three, leaving instructions to my stepmother to pass it on to Bob and me "when
we were old enough." I don't know what caused my stepmother to release it. Perhaps she thought, not without reason,
that she might outlive us all and could bury it with her yet.

The letter, never mailed, was written in pencil (didn't anybody in my family have a pen?) in Hazel's round, open hand on
the day before she died—April 12, 1929. It was addressed to
her parents, whom Hazel had just returned from visiting in
Eagle Rock, along with Lyda and another sister, who'd come
down from Bakersfield with her baby daughter. The sentences
ran on with the same girlish rush of the letters Hazel had written home on her trip East in 1912, when she enthused over the
noble domes of the nation's capital or the towers of Gotham.

Dear loved ones all.

I was so homesick to see you all and so happy to have
the privilege again and I just thought I would find a way
to show that I do appreciate all of you, what you have
been and are and do etc etc—but words seem slow in
coming and thoughts slower so the time passed so
quickly and I realized I had been receiving benefits all the
time while I contributed almost nothing to your joy and
comfort. The times together are so short and too soon
gone forever one wants to fill them full to overflowing. . . .

I just didn't have any visit with father, much to my re-

gret, and very little with mother it seems but oh I do
know that nobody ever had parents who wanted to do
more for their children. You gave us the right ideals and
aspirations and wore yourselves out trying to help us at-
tain them and I have been mean to ever criticize in anything. . . .

Oh my dear ones I do love you in spite of my stupidity. There is nothing I would not be willing to do for you
if I could see clearly the way and what God wants me to
do. If one could erase his mistakes as easily as he makes
them he could forget them more easily. God has shown
me His goodness so much thru my own family, my husband, children, friends and strangers, I should never
doubt His power to renew life and strength. In my teens
I received several wrong complexes, being very impres-
sionable which I can see now were brooded over too
much instead of being righted as they might have been
had I confided fully and relieved my mind of little fears.
I know a Christian should always be calm and serene. I
feel I cannot call myself a Christian when I don't feel
that God is leading me by the hand. I would rather have
that confidence, knowing that He has not cast me off,
than anything. Because of the crazy ideas I had at times
which destroyed the faith of my own little son and little
children who have seen me that way, I feel that I have
committed the unpardonable sin. My very fear of injur-
ing some one has largely made my life negative instead
of constructive as I desire.

The writing ended halfway down the yellowed page. There was
no signature. The unpardonable sin of doubt and despair. Neither Kennedy, Culver, Erskine, nor Harper was equipped, his-

torically or personally, to handle such dark feelings. Certainty was the lifeblood of the Elect, their salvation predestined by God's Grace in an act of faith as simple and pragmatic as hammering in a nail, as slicing an egg, as juicing an orange. For a good Calvinist, to doubt was as unthinkable as to swear or blaspheme or worship graven images. You didn't try to make sense of why some were saved and some were not. God's Will was as implacable as it was mysterious. Just lift the hammer or press down the wires or lower the lever, and don't gum up the works.

By the time I read my mother's letter, however, I'd been to college. I'd been through World War II. I'd lived for a decade under the thumb of my stepmother. I had long ago learned to be afraid of the dark. My grandma's nightly tuck-in echoed in my head long after she was gone, but the dark was too wide and too deep for the simple rhymes of

> *Sleep tight,*
> *Don't let the fleas bite,*
> *Wake up in the morning*
> *And do what's right.*

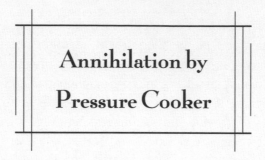

Annihilation by Pressure Cooker

FROM THE DAY we moved into the house on Walnut Street until the day I went away to college a decade later, I was trapped. Trapped like a piece of Swiss steak inside my father's favorite newfangled kitchen instrument, the pressure cooker. I would watch as he pounded the thin strips of raw beef with a wooden mallet, the head of which was scored in a grid on both ends. Wielded vigorously, the mallet reduced the muscled surface of the meat to pulp, as the strips flattened and thinned. Dad put the strips along with some sliced onions and canned tomatoes into the cooker and slipped the lid, with its mysterious top vent, under the lip of the pot so that the seal was tight. He turned up the heat until steam hissed from the open vent, then turned the heat down and narrowed the vent until the steam made a steady whistle, like the peanut whistle at the cement plant.

The pot attracted me because I was forbidden to use it unless my dad was there. It was a time bomb, a hand grenade, and you had to do everything exactly right or it might explode in your face and kill you, the way fifty years later a friend of mine was killed when she went to make breakfast and the stove blew up, setting her on fire and blackening her body to a cinder. Kitchens could be as risky as battlefields, and in my family the kitchen *was* a battlefield in our wars against flesh, poverty, and one another.

The nominal function of the pot was to cut down cooking time, which in the Depression seemed a good idea because it saved on gas. In our house there was no shortage of gas—it was forever trapped inside the plumbing of the Harper bowels and forever seeking release—nor of detailed discussions about its source and duration. If we could have figured a way to bottle it, we'd have been rich, like C. W. Post and W. K. Kellogg and all those other Elishas of Battle Creek who mapped an interior landscape as fraught with peril as any Bunyan's Pilgrim had to face.

So for us the pressure cooker's chief virtue was its ability to render the toughest material soft as cotton wadding. That saved chewing time and energy, as well as wear and tear on the dentures of the old and the vagrant choppers of the young. Our dietary Platonic ideal was water, and the pressure cooker did its bit in reducing solids to liquids. It turned beans to mush in a matter of minutes, squash to slush in a moment or two, spinach to a green puddle in seconds. When the war came on and the manufactories of such pots were retooled to make arms, a prewar cooker was all the more valued because it was thought to conserve vitamins, and vitamins were as vital to a Pilgrim's mess kit as prayer.

The first night I ever spent in the house on Walnut Street, I prayed hard, and when that didn't work, I cried so hard my dad had to bundle me up in a blanket and take me home. Home was not the double-storied square house with two blank eyes and a porched mouth and a long line of cement steps descending to the sidewalk like a lolling tongue. To the left of the mouth, a sign like a cartoonist's bubble announced: "Elizabeth Blake Harper, D.O." Home was Grandma and Grandpa H. in a stucco bungalow way across town from Dad and the wife who was not new to him but new to my brother and me.

If we could have kept our separate bivouacs at either end of town, we might have visited back and forth politely and peaceably. As I grew older, I might even have got used to staying overnight once in a while in the big house and not have to be taken home sobbing. As it was, no single encampment would have been big enough to contain the six of us without war.

My father had met the D.O., as my brother and I called her behind her back, through Grandpa H. when he came to visit his son in Riverside and, for future reference, checked out the osteopaths in town. Dr. Blake refused the widower each of the three times he popped the question in as many months, saying she was much too engaged professionally and financially to marry anyone, but he persisted. Years after his death, a bunch of penny postcards wrapped with a rubber band revealed that he'd courted her by postcard before they'd married. It was odd to read his penciled declarations that he missed her, my dad whose nearest approach to emotion was to clear his throat and say, like Popeye, "Blow me down." Eventually she surrendered, with conditions. They married the year after my mother died.

I have a few undated notebook pages, scribbled in pencil (of course) in the D.O.'s hand and titled "My Acquaintance with the Harpers." She gave in, she wrote, only after "*all circumstances* were considered and favorable agreement and reply made." Like my father, she chronically wrapped herself in the safety of generalized ambiguities and the passive voice. She itemized her reasons for agreement, the first of thousands of lists, thus:

Meryl's commitment
My commitment
Our contacts
Attitudes, wishes, statements of Gpa and Gma
Reactions to and by Us
Reactions to and by B & B

The only topic she filled in was "Meryl's commitment," quoting my father directly: "I want first of all to care for the children, then my parents, and then"—her own voice breaks through—"ME." He did admit, she goes on, that his father would often do things that were "hard to take" and that his mother did have "one little characteristic" but "you will *LOVE* her." She concludes this maddeningly obscurant document in the third person: "Thus began their acquaintance with, guess who, Dr. B.!"

It must have been quite a shock to her to be saddled with a girl of seven and a boy of eleven when Grandma H. became ill and the four of us moved into the house on Walnut Street. Bob and I knew next to nothing of Dr. B. except that we'd moved into the arms of the enemy. We didn't know that Dad took on a heavy mortgage of the house when the D.O. took him on. The house had belonged to her mother, a widow who'd lost her money and husband in the Crash and now ran a boardinghouse in another part of town. We called her Grandma Blake, and she didn't like us any better than the D.O. did. Eventually she came to live with us too, in order to die of a prolonged cancer. She spent her days doing crossword puzzles at the dining table and hated being interrupted; from her we learned that children should be neither seen nor heard.

Bob and I were instructed to call the D.O. "Mother," but it was hard going. In her late thirties, she was as homely as old maids were supposed to be, with marcelled hair and a bulbous nose and soft wet lips that I hated to kiss. Considering that this was 1934, either Dad and the D.O. were way ahead of their time in dividing up the domestic territory or else these were last desperate measures for them both. In addition to his teaching at the high school, Dad did all the shopping and cooking. This left the D.O. free to get on with her doctoring, which she transferred from an office in town to the house. The problem was, this woman who had never expected to marry or breed, and who had prostrated herself before the altar of osteopathy with the fervor of a novitiate before her abbess, was also put in charge of "the children."

The room between the parlor and the dining room became the D.O.'s examining room, equipped with an adjustable treating table next to an enamel table that held ominous instruments like stethoscopes and tongue depressors and blood-pressure pumps. Spinal adjustments were her specialty, and at the first sign of a sniffle or a sore throat, Bob or I would be summoned to the table for a neck crack, first to the right and then to the left, followed by a pull to the head straight on.

The floor of the dining room was covered with linoleum and the table with oilcloth. The windows were covered with green pull shades and framed with newspaper curtains. When the smudge pots got going in the orange groves, we simply crumpled the curtains up and threw them out. Opposite the windows was Dad's study, which when not occupied by the dying was a mortuary for pressed wildflowers, pinned butterflies, and formaldehyded frogs.

At the rear of the dining room were two doors. The swinging door to the left opened into a narrow corridor crammed with a gas water heater, a stove, and a sink lodged beneath a line of cupboards that ended in an enclosed pantry. That was the kitchen. The other door opened onto a screened porch with an icebox at the kitchen end and a toilet at the far end. The conjunction of kitchen and toilet was crucial in a house where outgo was more important than intake.

A mere corridor for a kitchen was okay with us, because my family had taken up arms against food as well as the flesh that required it. In the big house, even the simple pleasures of butter and eggs at Grandma's knee were gone. We were geared to a new regime where modern technology ruled. Castor oil, a concentrated prune pill, the old reliable pink rubber enema bag with its Vaselined tube, all were outmoded by the porcelain apparatus that took over the bathroom once a week for the adults to flush out their systems. Colonic irrigation was the last word in holy hygiene, the Amen to the benediction sung in unison by the Grape-Nuts, Shredded Wheat, Rice Krispies, Corn Flakes, Graham Crackers, Postum, and Ovaltine that congregated our shelves.

That all food tasted like dishwater was part of God's plan. Away with flavor, texture, taste. If all flesh is vanity, so is the food that feeds it. If spirit is all, who needs more than the Word of God? If God took on flesh in the body of Christ, He did so that we might shuck ours. Still, the flesh would not be denied its minute shivers of pleasure, even in the monotone of the bland leading the bland. Softly scrambled eggs were a triumph mixed with even softer scrambled brains. Soft white bread, toasted and resoftened in hot milk sprinkled with butter and sugar, was a treasured Sunday supper. Boiled fresh tongue, which I was allowed to strip of its thick pebbled skin and slice from tender tip to solid cartilaginous root, was delectable because of its velvet texture. Canned salmon, the only kind I knew, was satisfying because its bones were soft enough to chew. The divinity fudge that Grandma made at Christmastime was divine because of its Karo-white softness. And all year round, cornmeal mush, whether layered with ground meat and pitted black olives in a tamale pie or fried in rectangles and slathered with Log Cabin syrup or put in a bowl with a huge cube of butter topped with cinnamon and brown sugar and heavy cream, was everybody's favorite because it was mushy.

As any child knows, forbidden pleasures are best, and mine are vivid still. I was supposed to stay out of the dark pantry, so I snuck in when no one was around. I would pick out a box of Jell-O, red cherry over green lime, dip my fingers into the sweetened powder and lick them until the powder was gone. Or I would climb up to find an already opened bag of marshmallows, so that I could sneak one undetected. Or I would unscrew the top of a Welch's grape jelly jar and dip in the spoon I'd brought with me. Or I would open and sniff a mysterious jar labeled "Slippery Elm," in which pale bark floated in a strange-smelling liquid.

We gave no dinner parties. My parents had no friends. The church was our social circle, and though there were church dinners aplenty, to which every family contributed its bread-and-cheese casserole or rice pudding or store-bought rolls, the only festal occasions in our house were Thanksgiving, Christmas, and birthdays. At Thanksgiving and at Christmas, we had turkey. The white meat was bone dry and hard to swallow, so I asked Dad for dark and for extra skin, buttery and crisp and salty, and anyone who didn't want his was to save it for me. Best of all was the tail, which I would tear off in the kitchen afterward when no one was looking, setting my teeth into the sweet fat and licking my fingers one by one.

For birthdays we had fried chicken, as opposed to everyday rabbit, which was the cheapest of all meats because rabbits multiplied as quick as you could recite your multiplication tables. If we had roast chicken instead of fried, I got dibs on two parts, the wishbone and any embryonic egg yolks concealed in the chicken's cavity when it was cut open. A wishbone wish was good, but even better was finding a pair of yolks joined together like Siamese twins, a portent like the navel orange of God's blessing.

The D.O. was a Baptist, and while she set the precepts of our diet, Grandpa and Grandma H. did not recognize her doctrinal authority at our table or any other. For Calvinists, the education of children was a sacred charge: "to instruct those born ignorant of godliness in the purpose of eternity." Every morning after breakfast, Grandpa led the family in morning service. He opened the big family Bible at his place at the head of the table and read appropriate verses for the day. Then we turned our chairs around and knelt at them while he incorporated current events—Governor Landon's bid for the presidency or California's need for the Townsend Plan—into the day's prayers. At the end, we joined him in reciting "Our Father." We used the old form of the Lord's Prayer, meaningful to the times: "Forgive us our debts as we forgive our debtors." My brother would cheat and keep his eyes open, punching me in the ribs to make me squawk, but I closed my eyes tight. I longed to be saved, and until we came to live with the D.O. had never doubted that I was.

God, who looked just like my grandfather but with long white hair instead of the Kewpie-doll wisps that covered Grandpa's baldness, was listening and God was looking. God had X-ray vision and supersonic ears. He could see and hear every thought, every feeling, every pulse of every creature's mind and heart. Even though I'd been baptized and catechized, harmonized in choirs and sermonized in Sunday School and Daily Vacation Bible School, Sunday Morning Service and Sunday Evening Service, Wednesday Night Prayer Service and Young People's Christian Endeavor, still, God knew and I knew that I was damned.

I had to keep this knowledge secret from my grandparents, who foolishly believed that I'd be gathered in rejoicing with all the other sheaves. The D.O. knew better. When I said my nightly prayers, asking God to bless Grandpa and Grandma and Daddy and Mother and Brother, God knew I was asking Him to bless my real mother, not the D.O., and God knew that I was committing a sin by that lie. I knew that my stepmother hated us even as she tried not to and even though hate was a sin. I knew that the story of Hansel and Gretel was the story of Bobby and Betty, and I knew that the wicked stepmother and the wicked witch were one and the same, and that the D.O. would gladly have lost us in the forest or popped us in the oven if she could. Only she couldn't. She was stuck with us and we with her in the same cooker, and none of us knew how to turn it off before it exploded.

On Mother's Day at Calvary Church each year, children were given a red rose to pin on their clothes if their mother was alive and a white rose if she was dead. Bob and I wore our white roses like badges of honor, flaunting the fact of our "real" mother in the face of our fake one. If only the pair of us had presented a united front, we might at least have comforted each other, but we'd been polarized by gender from the start, the good girl and the bad boy. Grandpa H., who took me on his knee, took a razor strop to Bob to beat the rebellion out of him. Bob hated school as much as I loved it. He hated his younger sister, who got away with things he got blamed for. Once, in revenge, he wound his new electric train engine so thoroughly into my pigtails that they had to be cut into a Dutch bob. Once, also in revenge, I poured perfume over his head and it got in his eyes, and he threatened to tell unless I coughed up my nickel allowance to buy him off. He spent and I saved, so there was always a hoarded nickel to con me out of on one pretext or another.

We got on best during summer vacation, when Dad took us and my grandparents for a month to Long Beach and left the D.O. behind to do her doctoring. We rented a cheap little cottage in a row of them near a beautiful long stretch of public sand that was later wiped out in a hurricane. On Saturday nights we went to the Long Beach Pike and got soft ice cream from a machine that slipped a silky white ribbon into each cone. I would beg to go on the roller coaster, which extended spectacularly over the ocean from the pier, and Grandpa would tuck me in the seat beside him, pull down the bar in front of us, and remove his glasses so they wouldn't blow off in that first screeching, stomach-dropping descent. He took me on the Ferris Wheel, the Octopus, the Dodgem, the Loop-the-Loop, only one per visit because I got only one nickel and had to choose.

The best thing about summer vacation at Long Beach was that we were on vacation from the kitchen. We always ate Sunday noon dinner out. We went to a cafeteria, because that's where you got the best food for the least money, and you got to pick it out yourself without the embarrassment of waiters or other servitors. Once in a great while we would drive to L.A. to a Clifton's Cafeteria, which was an Ur-Disneyland of neon palm trees and real waterfalls and the Chapel of Gethsemane and a life-sized replica of Christ and the Apostles sitting down to a Last Supper of pot roast and mashed potatoes with a well in the middle for gravy, all for $1.95 and your money back if you weren't satisfied.

Or we joined one of the ongoing church picnics at Bixby Park. Long Beach was a gathering place for Bible Belt migrants, who used food to renew the ties that bind. Our numbers were such that picnic tables were organized by state—Kansas, Nebraska, Iowa, Illinois—hundreds of tables set up in the shade at noontime, and when we sang the Doxology it could be heard above the waves.

The place where we felt most free was the desert. I could feel my dad come alive and expand with every breath as he shifted gears on the hairpin turns of Box Spring Grade. At the summit we paused to eat our fried egg sandwiches beneath the pines, then dropped down into the breathtaking expanse of the Colorado or Mohave Desert to speed on roads straight as Cahuillan arrows toward the heat mirage shimmering on the horizon. Someone has said that American deserts and the Protestant conscience go together, both of them seared by the eye of God. Dad could recite the Latin and common names of every cactus, wildflower, bush, and tree, lingering in his litany over the vowels of *yucca* and *agave, ocotillo* and *chia, goose-foot* and *bladder sage*. His desert was a Bibleland of names: Yellow Star Thistle, Virgin's Bower, Our Lord's Candle, Joshua Tree. Tumbleweeds would blow across the road like wild free things, and I wanted never to go home.

At home, though, there were civil pleasures, if you loved to perform as I did. With my waist-length blond hair, I was always cast as an angel in the Christmas pageants that took place not only in front of Calvary's altar but in Riverside's municipal auditorium, with a cast of hundreds from all the schools of Riverside. One year a candle held by a fellow angel singed my hair, but Jesus saved and damped the flames.

I can't remember a time when I was not performing. Mine was the era of child stars like Shirley Temple and Freddie Bartholomew, and any kid worth his salt knew how to sing and dance. I remember singing "God Bless America" when I was six for Grandpa's Townsend Club, and not much later competing in an amateur hour, staged before the regular Saturday matinee at the Riverside Fox Theater, by singing all six verses of "My Name Is Solomon Levi." I had no notion it was about a Jewish secondhand clothes dealer, and I was puzzled why my pigtails and breathy little soprano fell flat.

Every group, every girls' club staged a skit, a musical, a pageant, several times a year, and I clamored to be in them all. The entire population of Riverside became players during the annual festival week, De Anza Days, which celebrated the Spanish who'd conquered the Indians before Father Junípero Serra converted them. Everyone but the real Indians, who'd been straitjacketed into the Sherman Institute, dressed in Spanish costume and paraded on horseback or in carriages and danced to mariachi bands playing "La Cucaracha" and "La Paloma."

Performing got me out of the house, or at least out of myself. Playing alone in front yard or back, depending on what scenery was wanted, I acted out all the girl parts of all the movies I'd seen with Grandpa. I was Heidi in Switzerland, cavorting with goats and eating cheese, I was Mary Queen of Scots going to her beheading with Hepburn cheekbones high, I was Jeanette MacDonald in the Rockies warbling "When I'm calling you-ooo-ooo" to Nelson Eddy. And when I ran out of movies,

I could swell into the grand operas I'd seen at the Riverside Opera House founded by none other than Madame Schumann-Heink, when she retired to the City of Oranges. I could be Humperdinck's Gretel or Verdi's Desdemona. Growing up with opera that way, I found it no more far-fetched than a Betty Boop cartoon.

And then there was the piano. Predestined by genetics and a full set of Kinsella Method music books, I was supposed to carry on my mother's good works at the pianoforte that stood like a memorial in the parlor. I turned out to be one of those rare pupils who truly loved to practice, because the piano was an escape, but whose finger skills improved with neither age nor experience. My teachers would always say, "Betty plays with a lot of feeling." It burned me up that the D.O., who played with no emotion whatsoever but who had strong fingers and hands, could play the piano far better than I.

With stiff fingers, Grandma H. every once in a while would cross her left hand over her right to play "In the Sweet By-and-By." I've forgotten how long in the sour present Grandma and Grandpa stuck it out with the D.O. before they moved out. Dad found a little cottage for them three blocks away, on Almond Street, with just enough yard for Grandpa to grow tomatoes and poinsettias and a few rows of corn, and with just enough kitchen for Grandma to cook applesauce and boil eggs. I stopped wetting my bed around the time they moved out, but I was still the victim of a nervous bladder that too often sent me home in tears at lunchtime to change clothes and squishy wet socks, then back to endure the taunts of schoolmates.

At best, the body was a shameful thing. From bedwetting I progressed to nosebleeding. Out of nowhere the flow would come, great red blobs staining my ironed dress, so that I'd have to lie down and press my index finger against my upper lip.

From nose to menstrual bleeding was an acceleration of bodily shame for which I was somehow responsible, since flesh was the source of sin and suffering and, like Christ, I was flesh and blood. I happened to be a flooder, for a full eight days and with no early warning system. Long before tampons were invented, I learned to wear two or three pads at a time, knowing that if I had no chance to change after an hour or two, the game was up, the flag was out, and shame would show.

The D.O. had lectured me about how lucky I was to be a modern girl, who could buy disposable aseptic absorbent pads. When she was a girl, women had to tear clean rags into strips and boil them in a pot to use over and over. I didn't feel lucky; I felt cursed by Eve's sin. I wasn't allowed to take a bath during the bleeding time, for fear of infection, and we had no shower. Keeping clean was a problem and keeping clean underwear a bigger problem. On a Sunday afternoon when my folks went off into the countryside to collect specimens for Dad's collection, I would sneak into the basement, soak my week's collection of bloodied cotton underpants in cold water in the sink, then boil them in a pot on the little two-burner stove. If it was a bright day, the pants could dry on the clothesline in half an hour. If it rained or the folks came back too soon, I would snatch them off the line and dry them secretly in my bedroom closet. Unlike Christ's, this blood offered no redemption.

I wasn't allowed to ride bikes, which were deemed too dangerous for girls. Nor, at sixteen, was I allowed to drive. I wasn't allowed to date a boy unless my parents had met him and we went with a chaperone. As a result, I had no dates except for chaperoned school proms and heavily supervised roller-skating parties in the back parking lot at church.

It was hard enough to see girlfriends. The D.O. disapproved of all my friends on principle. She would never explain why, she

would simply say, "I don't want you to see so much of . . ." Pat
Sides had been my best friend since junior high school. We were
a team, Sides and Harper, or, as I insisted, Harper and Sides,
and we did everything together at school. We wrote and starred
in the assembly skits, acted in the same school plays, edited the
yearbook together. But the D.O. disapproved of Pat's parents,
who lived on the other side of town, the better side, when they
were not abroad. Pat's mother was an artist and her father a
mining engineer, and they went off to live in exotic parts of the
world like Cyprus or Brazil while Pat's grandmother took care
of her in Riverside. When her parents came home, they moved
with an artistic crowd who smoked and drank and did not attend church regularly. They were Episcopalians anyway, and
Episcopalians were notorious because they smoked and drank.
The fingers and lips of Pat's mother were stained yellow with
tobacco.

I was in torment every time Pat invited me to a movie or to
her house for dinner. I couldn't go anywhere without the D.O.'s
permission, so I would rehearse my lines over and over, changing the intonation, screwing up the courage to walk down the
stairs and face her. There was no predicting what I'd find—a
sullen pout or an angry brow, a cold silence or a hot tirade.
"And when do I get to go to the movies? Who ever asks me to
go out after I've slaved for you week after week? Who ever
thinks about me?" I thought about the D.O. all the time, but
not in the way she wanted. And there was no way to respond
except to run to my room, sit on my bed with its pink dimity
spread beneath a framed reproduction of *Pinkie*, look at myself
in the mirror of the vanity table with its matching pink skirt beneath the framed reproduction of *Blue Boy*, and sob until the
well went dry.

Repetition increased the D.O.'s contempt and my hopelessness. No matter what I did, I was going to lose. I had fantasies of running away to Aunt Lyda's, but I was too practical to try it. I had no money and no way to get any, certainly not enough for a bus ticket. I couldn't get far on the nickel allowance that was mine until high school, when it rose to a dime. Some policeman would bring me back, sheepish with my little hobo stick and handkerchief filled with peanut butter and jelly sandwiches, and the D.O. would thunder at me and send me to bed.

Bob had made his escape from Riverside the day he turned eighteen, signing up for the Marines in April 1941. He would come home on leave from boot camp at Camp Pendleton in San Diego and tell us laughingly how he had to scrub the latrines with a toothbrush for fifteen hours a day. I envied him. He got himself a girl, too, and eloped with her to Las Vegas, bringing her around to meet the folks on his way back to camp. He needn't have bothered. The D.O. puckered her lips and snorted and fumed. Gwen stood on the sidelines in her big picture hat, with an orchid on her tight-fitting powder-blue suit, while the D.O. grumbled that it was a crying shame they'd *had* to get married and at least they should have gotten married in a church, and good governor, Bob, if you have to smoke, smoke that cigarette outside, not in my house. With my gangly frame, I envied Gwen in her suit and hat and shapely legs in high-heeled white shoes. At last Bob had got a Vargas girl of his very own, just like the ones in the magazines he kept under his mattress until the D.O. found them and threw them out.

What Gwen remembers from that visit is finding me bent over the treadle sewing machine, sobbing the while, my tears wetting the material and rusting the needle. Crying was a permanent condition, like Dad's postnasal drip or my year-round hay fever that the D.O. attributed to my not dusting my room. Not long ago I found a little black notebook of the D.O.'s in yet one more box of family junk. It is filled with penciled reminders to herself, listed, as always:

> Bob is bad.
> Betty musn't cry so much.

I cried upstairs, downstairs, all around the house. I cried so often nobody paid any attention, including me, and I couldn't stop because I knew that until I left that house, I was the D.O.'s prisoner and she could bully me as she chose. Tears were the steam bobbing the vent in the pressure cooker lid, lest greasy little pieces of me explode over the kitchen walls.

It took a movie to make me see what a wimp I was. I saw *The Ox-bow Incident* with Pat in our senior year, and I couldn't get over how bravely one of the teenage boys had talked back to his bullying father, until Pat said, "It sure took him long enough." Talking back was a possibility I'd never entertained. But one day, when the D.O. was complaining about Grandma H., I turned on her in a fury that surprised us both. "Don't ever talk about my grandmother again. Not ever." The D.O. reared back as if punched, opened her mouth like a fish, then closed it. I knew and she knew I'd opened a vent she couldn't close.

I realize now that the D.O. cowed me because I was cowable. In a house where all emotions but hers were taboo, she had free run of the range, and I feared her tantrums as I feared natural disasters like forest fires and earthquakes. I feared her because whatever happened was my fault.

In my apartment in New York I once made vinegar, in a two-liter Italian green glass jar designed for that purpose, with a spigot at the bottom and an open mouth at the top covered with cheesecloth held by a rubber band. I was using a purchased "mother," which had only to be fed with fresh white wine from time to time so that she would form the layers of brown leathery skin on top of the liquid that would turn the wine to vinegar without its going bad. Trouble is, I put the jar in a dark cupboard and forgot about it for a couple of years, and when I remembered to give it a look, the "mother" had grown into a monstrous multilayered slime covered with blue-green mold that entirely filled the jar. Inside the jar, the wine was gone, the "mother" had consumed every drop, but it was hardly the fault of the wine that I had all "mother" and no vinegar.

In the D.O.'s house the only thing that wasn't my fault, or Bob's fault, was the war. We first heard about the bombing of Pearl Harbor when we turned on the Zenith in our dining room one sunny December noon after church. What had been happening in Europe had been no concern of ours. Most of the evils in the world could be attributed to Franklin D. Roosevelt or John L. Lewis or both, and we knew that Roosevelt had been conspiring to drag us America Firsters, despite the efforts of our hero Lindbergh, into the war in Europe where we had no business at all. But Hawaii was different. Hawaii belonged to us.

Bob was glad when Pearl Harbor was bombed, because he was eager to ship out for action in the South Pacific. You couldn't get farther away from Riverside than that. My war was the romance of him coming home on leave in his snappy khaki uniforms with the thick leather belts and polished buttons and his brimmed Marine hat set on the back of his head at a slant to match his grin and cigarette. Now and then he would bring home a buddy unlucky enough to have no place else to go. My parents suffered the tobacco smoke with grim faces, but I couldn't get enough of their rough talk, their rough khakis, and their horror stories about the evil Japs. Bob would tease me by calling me Torpedo Betty after the Jap twin-engine bombers they nicknamed Big Butt Bettys. But he was more at ease with me now. He'd come into his own on Guadalcanal, where schoolwork and grades didn't matter and bravado did, where not getting killed was better than the best report card.

My war was strictly racial and solely against the Japs. The Germans, the French, the Poles, the Brits, none of them appeared on our maps, which looked west across the Pacific to the East. If someone came from the Old World, they came from China or Japan. There were many Japanese in my high school, and when my friends Tomiko Ito and Tommy Hirakowa disappeared from our classrooms overnight, we were told that they'd been removed for their own safety to an unspecified place remote from the coast. There were daily rumors of Japanese invasion somewhere along the Pacific coastline, sometimes by submarine, sometimes by airplane or balloon. We taped our windows with blackout shades in preparation for air attack. Our newspaper printed instructions for "Dimout Dos and Don'ts," enforced by block wardens, who advised us what to do in case a fire was started by fifth columnists or a demolition bomb fell in our block or a poison gas attack threatened our town. Air-raid sirens warned us when to drop everything and head for the basement with blankets and pillows until the all clear sounded, the same way fire-alarm bells at school had warned us when to hide under our desks during earthquake drills.

Bob's was not the soothing nighttime voice of H. V. Kaltenborn on the radio. Bob told of being on night patrol in the jungle when, sensing that an unfamiliar body had fallen

into step behind him, he turned suddenly and plunged his bay-
onet through a Jap dressed in the uniform of a U.S. Marine. He
brought home snapshots of his buddies kicking around a Jap
head, like a football. He also brought home a first-class case of
malaria, because the troops had got to Guadal before Atabrine
did, and he spent a week with chills and fever and delirium on
the living-room couch, reliving the horror of battle behind
closed doors. One day he was at the icebox looking for something cold to drink when the D.O. came up behind him and he
whipped around with his hand ready to strike. "For Christ's
sake, Mom, don't ever sneak up behind me that way," he said.
"I could have killed you." "Don't you take the Lord's name
in vain, Robert Leroy Harper," she said, "or I'll have you
whipped."

I was prepared for invasion by Japanese soldiers, whose first
act would be to rape and mutilate every white teenage girl they
could find. I'd seen the movies. I knew what monsters Japs
were, equipped with squinty eyes and bucktoothed grins as
they dove their kamikaze planes straight into the decks of our
aircraft carriers and into the heart of their Emperor. Long after
the war was over, I had a recurrent nightmare that the Japs had
invaded Riverside and I had to escape. It was night and I was
alone in the house, waking with a start in my pink-and-blue
bedroom to hear voices jabbering in the darkness outside. The
trick was to run downstairs, through the dining room, out the
back porch, down the stairs, through the basement, and into
the crawl space without being seen. Maybe my best bet was to
run from my bedroom into the bathroom at the end of the hall,
crawl through its window onto the half roof of the back porch,
let myself down over the edge, and drop from there to the
ground. It wasn't a bad drop, and even if I turned or broke an
ankle, I could still drag myself into the crawl space. Even today

I can feel my heart pound as I lie squeezed between dirt and joist, watching through a narrow latticed vent in the wall the boots of men running past, shouting in excitement as they hunt me down.

Everything happened so fast after Uncle Sam went to war. It seemed that one year we were celebrating the first airmail flight in Riverside County and a mere three years later we were cheering on F-4F Wildcat fighters over Guam. One year I was holding back tears because nobody wanted to dance with a wallflower like me at the Soirée Dansante, and the next year I was jitterbugging with pint-sized soldier boys at the USO and was voted pinup girl by the 823rd Antiaircraft Battalion at Camp Haan. One year I'd never been kissed and the next I was fighting off boys in Army khaki or Navy white who were shipping out and had nothing to lose by going too far.

At my farewell senior assembly in junior high, in a blue dress I'd made on the Singer at home, I sang "There'll be blue birds ovah the White Cliffs of Dovah" to acknowledge our new Allies. In my first year at high school, we staged war-bond rallies and donned overalls as Victory Girls to harvest onions and grapes in fields that draftees had left shorthanded. At home, we wrote V-mail letters and tended Victory Gardens. We clumped tinfoil into balls and saved bacon fat in cans and colored white oleomargarine butter-yellow and stopped putting sugar in our coffee or gas in our tanks and shut our mouths to prevent loose lips from sinking ships. But as teenage girls we knew that nothing we did really counted, no matter what Uncle Sam said, because we were girls.

At eighteen we could join the Waves or Wacs or Waafs, although my parents believed, and many of us did too, that only prostitutes and dykes did that. Older women could become

Rosie the Riveters; Pat's mother became a tank designer for the Food Machinery Corporation. But younger girls, girls in their summer dresses and bobby socks and pigtails, could do nothing but stay just as they were, slide down that cellar door, climb up that apple tree, and pretend that bombs were not falling and mortars not blowing men to bits—elsewhere. And for that very reason, I was for the first time truly glad to be a girl.

From movies of Nazi storm troopers torturing their victims, I knew I could never be a spy, a member of the Resistance, a Freedom Fighter, because I would spill every bean at the first touch of a lit cigarette to the wrist, the first tug of a fingernail from a finger. Nor could I imagine myself hurling a grenade at a pillbox or diving into a foxhole under machine-gun fire. In any scene of bombardment, I was one with the women and children huddled in underground shelters in London, or in a village cellar in Normandy, a tenement in Rome, a rice paddy in the Philippines.

I knew that who got killed and who didn't had nothing to do with personal bravery or morality. Victims were hostages to fortune, luck, a bomb's caprice, death's whim, God's Will. I understood in my gut the helplessness of civilians in war, as they listened to the whine of the bomb overhead and more intently to the silence after, until they could breathe with relief because their neighbors had been hit instead of themselves. I laughed as hard as anyone at Hitler jokes, doing raspberries "right in der Führer's face," but he was not a caricature to me. I knew what it was to be subject to a tyrant's whim, even if the domain was as small as a kitchen.

Still, there was no bridging the gap between civilian and combatant, despite the stories Bob and his buddies told, despite the battle scenes in *Life* painted by servicemen or photographed

by war correspondents, whose black-and-white prints had all
the reality of silent-movie stills. It was all too much, too extreme, too remote. Whatever was happening wasn't happening
to us. No photos of dead American servicemen graced the
pages of an American newspaper or magazine or the frames of
a newsreel until late in the war. We conspired in the myth that
although our boys were often missing in action, they didn't
have corpses. They just disappeared into the wild blue yonder
to reappear as a star in some Gold Star Mother's window.

That's why what happened, later on in the war, to the Reverend Ezra James Egly of our Calvary Presbyterian Church was
such a shock. His own sons weren't old enough to fight, but
Pastor Egly had embraced all of Calvary's boys as his own. He
often wept openly as he read aloud letters in which they swore
there were no atheists in foxholes. If they swore different, they
wouldn't have bothered to write, because nobody would have
believed them. So how did the Reverend Egly come to hang by
a rope strung from the top of one of the organ pipes in the
church basement, where the caretaker found him one night? It
was a sneak attack. Our flock had been betrayed, as our boys
had been at Pearl Harbor. The smiling communicant in your
pew could be a member of the fifth column. No one was to be
trusted. There was no sure Place.

When it came time to pick a college, I wanted to go as far
from Riverside as I could get, so I begged to go to the University of California at Berkeley. My parents opted for Occidental
because it was close and it was Presbyterian. Pomona College
was our compromise and, fortunately, Pat wanted to go there
too. Best of all, Pat had a car, a used Ford pickup truck painted
red. Gas and tire rationing didn't let her use it much, but it
spelled hope and freedom and escape, three different words for
the same thing. The cooker had finally blown its lid, and I ex-

ploded in a jet of steam. As we sped along Route 66 with the wind blowing through our hair, laughing so hard we sometimes had to stop the car, we knew from scalp to toe how great it was even in the midst of war to be young and alive and on the road to nowhere but tomorrow.

Blitzed by
Bottle Caps and Screws

I RAN BAREFOOT lickety-split across the lawn of Harwood Court in my spiffy new red-polka-dot pajamas in the cool night, slipped on the wet grass, skidded on my butt into a camellia bush, and it didn't matter at all that I'd twisted my ankle and stained my rayon bottom a bright indelible green. There was a heaven after all, and I was in it.

It was the fall of 1944, and the whole campus felt like a pajama party, with an unending supply of Ritz crackers and pimiento cheese and bottles of Coke. Every night, in one dorm room or another, we read aloud the dirty parts of *Gone with the Wind* and passed around the lone bottle opener, as valuable as a Zippo lighter, since all such metal objects, along with Lucky Strike Green, had gone to war. Because Coke contained caffeine and God knows what other stimulants, it had been taboo in my house, where even ginger ale was permitted only for upset stomachs. To be able to open any kind of soft drink with an experienced flip of the wrist was to open the mouths of new worlds. In comparison to the other girls, I was a yokel out of *Li'l Abner*, and after my prolonged confinement, I burst forth with the force of Kickapoo Joy Juice kept too long in the jug.

For me, no campus revolution was bigger than the change in what and how I ate. At table I was like a child who knew how to walk but had to learn to run. My friends teased me without mercy when they discovered that I was always the last to clean my plate because I was still Fletcherizing my meat with fifty chews per bite. They would count down in unison: "Ten, nine, eight, seven, six, five, four, three, two, one, SWALLOW." I tried to explain that I'd never had meat that you couldn't cut with a spoon, except at Pat's, where her grandmother served delicious little lamb chops that you could eat in a single bite. But with practice I improved and became such a speedy chewer in my first semester that I won a contest in the spring by stuffing a whole pie in my mouth before I swallowed.

For the first time in my life, I drank coffee, black and at every meal, despite Grandpa H.'s warnings that my skin would turn sallow. But I wasn't ready to defy family prohibitions against tobacco and alcohol. Because of Pat I'd been accepted by the "fast" gang of frosh girls. Most of them smoked and drank beer and, at places where they could use their fake IDs, cocktails. I didn't know how to do any of those things and didn't want to learn. Besides, I couldn't afford cigarettes or booze on my dollar-a-month allowance, which would buy a weekly lime and Coke and no more.

I waited tables in the college dining rooms and at a local eatery called the Mish and jerked sodas at the Student Coop, but my earnings were a drop in the bucket. Dad had driven a taxi in the summer to pay my tuition, but there was no money for books, let alone extras. Every time I bought a bag of french fries, I worried. Fortunately Claremont weather allowed me to

wear sandals and a raincoat through most of the winter, and
Pat sometimes let me borrow one of the sweaters Gran had knit
her, but I felt shabby. I hated being poor. Blue jeans helped even
that score, and nobody fought fiercer than I for the right to
wear them.

Try to imagine a time, dear reader, when college women
were not allowed to wear trousers of any kind outside their
rooms, and certainly not in their classrooms. These were the
days when professors addressed their female students as
"Miss." Our regulation costume was loose sweaters, pleated
skirts, bobby socks, and penny loafers for day wear, silk stock-
ings (or leg makeup with a line drawn up the back for a seam)
and heels and a dress-up dress for dinner, served by student
waiters at candlelit tables in Harwood Court. At dinner each
Miss was to be an exemplar of Gracious Living, as defined by
our Dean of Women, Miss Gibson, to keep the home fires burning with a civilized flame.

But having escaped my stepmother's hearth, I was wildfire,
eager to incinerate all rules and regulations that threatened my
new freedom. I organized a sit-in, or wear-in, of blue jeans on
campus, first outside the classroom and then in the classroom
itself. Having won the right to pants, we now insisted on wearing our cotton plaid shirts outside them instead of tucked into a
belted waistband. A gang of us often hitchhiked in shirttails
and jeans down to Laguna Beach for a day in the sand. It was
our patriotic duty to hitchhike, we explained, to save on gas
and tires; besides, guys hitchhiked everywhere. I began to be
called in regularly to the housemother's office at Harwood
Court to explain our latest subversion of Gracious Living.

In the middle of a war that stamped women as sexual inferi-
ors as blatantly as it stamped the few men on campus 4-F, we
were fighting a battle for sexual equality against a battalion of

deans and housemothers and faculty wives wielding parietal rules more appropriate to the time of the Spanish-American War than the second global one. We were supposed to be in our dorms by 10:30 on weeknights and 12:30 on Saturdays. We had to get permission to leave campus overnight, were unenforceably but officially forbidden to consume alcohol at any time, were required to make our beds and keep our rooms clean. Men students had no chores and no rules whatsoever, except that they were not allowed to bring women into their rooms. This kind of sexual discrimination galled us, especially in matters of food and drink.

The men ate in Frary Hall, famed for the Orozco fresco that dominated the Spanish mission interior of the dining room by means of a giant male nude, the figure of Prometheus squeezed into an arch and scowling at the fact that his genitalia, like those of Michelangelo's Sistine Christ, had been excised by a genteel brush. If the men's hall was grand, so was their food. Team sports were the excuse that allowed male students to get real meat—steak, roasts, chops—instead of the eternal gray casseroles of sludge that were our lot. And they could drink alcohol wherever they chose.

The only food we shared on equal terms was ice cream, the gift of some hungrily remembering alumnus who bequeathed an eternal supply of ice cream of good quality with a choice of three flavors, vanilla, chocolate, or strawberry, to be offered at every meal but breakfast. So grateful were we for ice cream after sludge that within six months most of us had good reason to wear shirttails outside our hard-to-button jeans. (Flies were buttoned instead of zipped because zippers were made of metal, and that metal too had gone to war.)

Then as now our regalia was full of paradox. We donned blue jeans, but we also curled our hair and powdered our noses and rubied our lips. When I think of the time I spent, from junior high onward, putting up my hair, I could cry. At the time, though, straight hair was unthinkable. If we were blond, we wore high pompadours like Betty Grable, to match our lipsticked mouths, but the rest of our hair had to fluff in waves. Hair was yet one more female curse, and so each night I sighed and wet the ends of each strand and curled it into a tight circle and pinned it to my scalp next to hundreds of other tightly wound strands.

No effort was too great to land our man, and what else were we here for? I'd just met and fallen half in love with one of the handsomest men I've ever known. He was a pilot in the Army Air Corps whom I'd met on a blind date arranged by an older girl, a junior, who was dating one of his buddies. He was blond, brown-eyed, square-chinned, and as clean-cut nice as he was tall. I spent a weekend once with his pilot buddies and their girls, some of them already married to each other. We drove all night from Claremont across the Mohave Desert to Pearblossom, where the family of one of them had a cabin. The boys slept in one bedroom, the girls in another, and we sat together in front of a big fireplace in the room in between to sing songs like "Don't Fence Me In." But what I liked most was sitting on Bruce's lap in the crowded back seat of the car on the night drive across the desert, resting my head and wavy hair on his chest and pretending to be asleep so that I could hear his heart beat and feel his jaw resting on my head. A sure Place.

When he was stationed at March Field, he came a few times to Pomona to a dance or for an afternoon's walk. But after he was sent to Boca Raton, I lost track because he stopped writing letters and my friend said he'd met a girl in Florida. I didn't know he'd been shot down and killed on his first mission in the

Pacific until two or three months after it happened. I wanted to play the heroine of tragic romance but couldn't, because he'd already left me behind. Still, he was the most beautiful guy I ever saw and he died young.

The war ended, at least the only one that counted, the one against the Japs, in the summer between my freshman and sophomore years, when I was working for the Riverside Recreation Department's craft workshop in the basement of the municipal auditorium. Mostly we taught schoolkids how to tool leather and tint photographs and carve linoleum blocks for prints, but once a week our students were German and Italian prisoners of war shipped in from a camp outside town in their gray prison uniforms for a change of scene. They made little effort to tool leather, but they rolled their eyeballs and leered a lot. One day in August, the excitable high school teacher who managed the auditorium called me over to look at the headlines of the newspaper he was reading. "Would you look at that," he said. "An atom bomb! Do you know what that means?" I didn't. But no more did I know the meaning of what he'd shown me the day before, with the same kind of moral intensity. "Would you look at that," he'd said, displaying a circle of white rubber taken from some eighth-grade schoolboy's wallet left carelessly behind. "Can you imagine! Do you know what that means?" I registered the shock he demanded, but I hadn't the foggiest.

The vets returned in a trickle, then a wave. At Pomona we girls had been running the campus, occupying the posts of leadership, staging the shows, editing the newspaper, practically managing the football team. Overnight we were displaced by all those guys we'd been waiting for by not sitting under the apple tree with anybody else but them. Overnight we were busted, not from officer to private, but to comfort woman.

There were obvious wounded. Guys with one real leg and one false, guys with scarred faces and arms, guys with dark glasses where their eyes had been. There were a great many wounded whose bodies were intact but whose psyches were damaged in ways we knew nothing about. I had a blind date with one of the first vets back, set up by a senior whose Army vet fiancé knew his friend dug blondes. But I came down with flu and had to cancel, which I thought bad luck until I learned that the blonde he got instead of me he'd tried to rape. The weekend after that, he drove his car up to Mount Baldy, got roaring drunk, and cruised off a cliff on the way down. Later, they found a suicide note in his dorm.

While we had marked time, time had marked them, marked even the men who hadn't seen combat, who'd had to fight boredom instead of bayonets. No one escaped guilt. Men were guilty if they hadn't fought overseas, they were guilty if they'd fought and survived. And girls were guiltiest of all, for not being in the flesh what the men imagined they had left behind, those movie-perfect images of purity and innocence that were counterparts of their own lost selves. We tried hard to comfort them for all their losses. We put their heads in our laps and stroked their hair and let them cry. We listened to their war stories and their tales of comic snafus and their broken laments and never once dreamed of asking for equal time. We were not equal. We had done nothing. We had nothing to tell.

And like men from the beginning of time, these soldier men wanted us virgin pure but ready for carnal knowledge. I had a year's grace, because in my sophomore year I was pursued and pinned, fraternity style, to a vet who was the equivalent of a

Christian Endeavor youth leader. He neither smoked nor drank nor swore, but came out of the Army as squeaky clean as he went in. Before the war, he'd worked as one of the army of cartoonists at Disney Studios, and now he sold us signed copies of Mickey Mouse and Donald Duck suitable for framing. At parties where other vets were tanking up and falling down, he ostentatiously drank milk by the quart. Despite the ridicule of my pals, I was happy to join him in milk drinking. I was less happy to join him in any heavy-duty activity below the neck.

Like other vets, he was horny. Unlike other vets, he was patient. My gang lived that year in an old-fashioned three-story frame house with a front and side porch and a live-in housemother. Just before curfew, which had been extended to 11:30 on weeknights, the dark porches would be clogged with couples gone surreally silent, girls pushed up against the walls as if the guys were using them to keep the building from collapse. The lights snapped on at 11:25 sharp, to reveal faces with hair askew, lipstick smeared, men slipping into the shadows, girls staggering through the front door and up the stairs to collapse on beds in fits of giggles and exhaustion.

We wore fluffy angora sweaters in pastel colors that year and wondered why guys couldn't keep their hands off us, off *them*—the rounded nippled breasts—searching for them under sweaters, under bras, with palms and fingers and lips. They searched us as we necked on grassy lawns and sandy beaches and chintz settees and in the front and back seats of cars. On a sunny afternoon my vet and I necked in the empty bleachers of the Greek theater in the middle of the scrub area of oaks and cactus we called the Wash, and for the first time I let him take my sweater off and then my bra. When he wanted to undo my skirt I made him stop, but I let him take my hand and put it on the lump in his trouser front. He wanted to feel me up, but I didn't want to feel him. I didn't want equal time. I was terrified of sex.

When my vet's patience finally ran out, after he'd driven me all the way to Riverside because Grandpa H. had just died, and we necked in the moonlight at Fairmount Park and I still wouldn't go all the way, he took back his pin and I stopped drinking milk. The preferred beverages were Acme beer in quart bottles (for parties a wooden keg) and demijohns of Gallo wine that you opened by screwing off the caps and poured into paper cups with ice and soda water, so that you could get through large quantities of it without vomiting. At first I liked the wine and soda better than the beer because beer was bitter and made you burp. But I knew as little about wine as I knew about sex, and after a wine party with Pat and a group of vets, I lay on my back on my bed with the whole room gyrating and a voice from outer space saying over and over, "I am not drunk."

Once I started, I drank only to get drunk. Booze helped fill the gap between the vets, who knew everything, and us, who knew nothing. Yet try as we might to match them drink for drink, we couldn't. They kept filling our glasses with one rotgut or another to loosen our conjugations, but there was only a hairline inflection between loosening up and throwing up. Or passing out. By doing the latter regularly, I learned what too much booze did to girls. Only later did I learn what too much booze did to men.

As I look back now on the primacy of our drinking rituals, I think sex was a cover. What both sides wanted was a way to mask our mutual embarrassment at having nothing to say because we had no language in common, and screwing wasn't going to change that.

Our smoking rituals were the same. My friends had taught

me to smoke, finally, when I won the role of Sabina in Thornton Wilder's *The Skin of Our Teeth* and had to smoke onstage. This was the role Tallulah Bankhead had made famous on Broadway, but I'd never heard of Tallulah and had terrible trouble acting like a seductive sexpot who didn't cough when she inhaled. I didn't tell my parents I'd got the lead, because I didn't want them to come to a performance and see me smoking. But the ritual went hand in hand with drinking, and I was soon up to two packs a day. Smoking was about hands the way drinking was about mouths. Unzipping the cellophane and undoing the foil, hitting the bottom of the pack on the side of your hand, shaking out a cig, placing it between your first and second fingers, waiting for a light, holding gently the extended hand that held the lighter, taking the first puffs to make sure the end was lit, inhaling deeply and breathing out slowly to watch the smoke fill the air between you and your companion smoker, tapping the glowing end lightly, watching the ash fall. For some of us, it was better than sex.

Most of us were too ignorant to be honest about sex. Even for GIs who'd learned the rudiments abroad, wartime sex was very different from civilian sex, which seemed annoyingly to involve other things like love and commitment and endless conversation and endless cigarettes. The vets helped teach girls like me to hide our emotions behind sandbags, to shoot down silly notions about love and romance. They had returned from the Real World as if from the dead, as if to expose how tinselly, how phony was the little crepe-paper world we'd wrapped ourselves in. Even learning, which I'd exploded into as a freshman, studying Plato with the avidity I'd once applied to the Bible, seemed a waste of time. I went to fewer and fewer classes, just enough to get that Purple Heart, a Phi Beta Kappa key, because I couldn't stop being the good student even though I no longer

believed that grades meant anything. At nineteen I was beginning to worry that I had no passion in me when I first saw Paul
outside Holmes Hall, dappled by the shade of a sycamore like
an elongated faun in preppy clothing, and worried no more.

I fell in love the way girls did in movies, from the way he
looked, tall and lean with jutting brows, slanted pixie eyes and
tilted smile, his shoulders slightly hunched in a gray-blue crew-
neck sweater over a button-down shirt, white buck shoes beneath gray flannels. On that campus, he was exotic. I was used
to boys in jeans and lumber-jacket shirts and Army-issue fa-
tigues. I was used to, and mighty tired of, men being either
jocks or flits. We used to complain about the macho types you
loved to kiss but couldn't talk to and the queers you loved to
talk to but couldn't kiss. To find a good looker who was also
smart and talented and passionate about art, and at the same
time vulnerable because he'd been wounded by the war, well,
the combination was irresistible, and who was I to resist?

Paul belonged to the literary set, a tight coterie of writers
and would-be writers, whom I both envied and resented for the
certainty of their opinions about the Great Works of Literature,
to which they laid claim. Within that set, he belonged to the
Novelist, an excitingly fun and unconventional tomboy who
was destined to be, none of us doubted, America's first female
Hemingway, and who ended up writing nothing at all. When
they broke up, Paul took up with me, a mere philosophy major
who had no opinions about Great Works I'd scarcely heard of.

I read fiction the way Grandma had taught me to read the
Bible, piecemeal, as isolated statements taken out of context, as
if whatever was printed on a page expressed God's literal truth
or the search for it, sentence by sentence, page by page. Pat

read everything, like her mother, and she knew the names of
books and authors and how to talk about them. She also had
an ease in writing that was my despair. She could toss off in an
hour an English paper that I struggled with for a day and a
night. Writers are born, not made, I'd decided, although when I
met Paul, I was ready to be reborn.

I was not a Writer, but I listened and became an eager
Reader as I began to finger the works themselves, falling in love
simultaneously with Mann and Gide and Proust and Joyce. I
was an instant convert, finding for the first time in fiction the
depth of meaning I had looked for in philosophy, until I got
stranded in logical abstractions. When I fell in love with Paul, I
fell in love with literature, in sickness and in health, for better
and for worse, and no matter what course the narrative took, I
never fell out of love with either.

Paul was an apostle of a new faith that hit me as it hit Saul
on the road to Damascus. His set included a couple of teachers
as well as students, teachers who were also just back from the
wars, real men who were light-years away from the genteel lady
high school teachers of Wordsworth and Keats. And at the center of this circle was a writer truly modern, a great European, a
Nobel Prize winner, who was alive and well and living, pecu-
liarly enough, in Hollywood—Thomas Mann. *The Magic
Mountain* was their Bible, as taught by a charismatic professor
appropriately named Angell, who actually knew Mann personally, was writing a book about him, worshipped him as the
writer-seer we'd sought to explain the horrors of the Real
World as it was happening, now. Mann wrote the kind of fiction even I could read, because I read it as if it were a biblical
epic, and for the first time Europe became a real place and its
conflicts helped explain a real war.

Paul's commitment to literature as an art, a sacred text, was religious. It had saved him in the war, he said. Before this altar I was a willing acolyte, with Paul as my priest. It was tremendously exciting to find a new religion after the loss of the old, and a new god. The literary disciples met in one or another professor's house on equal terms, because what little difference there was in age between them was wiped out by the shared experience of the war and by a shared mission. To them Art was no ivory tower but a mode of moral action, an activist's salvation from the chaos of war and the newly unleashed terrors of the atom bomb. Joe Angell had been in an intelligence unit of the Air Force and knew a lot of inside stuff about government plans for the bomb. He never divulged any secrets but he made apocalypse a felt possibility. He also made seizing the moment the only right way to go, and when we all got drunk together at his house, we got drunk on good bourbon and on wine that you had to open with a corkscrew.

Paul was the star of this group. He was the best writer, the most intense, the most persuasive, the most talented, the most committed. Because he'd hated athletics as a fat boy, he'd specialized early, writing and printing his own neighborhood newspaper as a teenager, excelling in English classes and flunking math, scorning what he was not good at to compete keenly in what he was. He thought my philosophy courses absurd, my ignorance of literature pathetic, but he welcomed a bright and wide-eyed disciple. I gave him practice in the role of the teacher he wanted to be and would soon become. If not for the war, he would have been a journalist, but the war turned him serious and gave him a classroom mission that his father decried, because it made no money. His mother understood. "I always thought that if Paul hadn't become a teacher he would have made a good preacher," she said once, "although I couldn't vouch for what he'd preach."

Paul had extra glamour for me because he wasn't poor. He came from Pasadena. He had a car. He would take me out not just to Lucy's in Ontario to eat a bargain dinner of garlic bread, red-sauced spaghetti, and cheap red wine, but to the far more costly Sagehen on Route 66 to drink old-fashioneds or martinis and eat shrimp cocktails and thick steaks with baked potatoes. And throughout dinner he would talk, about literature and art and politics. His father was a big-time corporate lawyer who became head of Pomona's Board of Trustees. He had an older brother who'd preceded him at Pomona and was already in Harvard graduate school getting his Ph.D. Paul came from another world, another class, and I kept wanting to give him little presents to express my gratitude. "You're funnier than Pat," he told me once, and I said, "That's odd, because our humor's very much the same." "Not funny ha-ha," he said, "funny peculiar."

Paul was funny ha-ha. Before he'd gone to war, he'd edited the college humor magazine and enacted the role, with another chubby friend, of class clown. The war slimmed him and trimmed him and sharpened his wit. He was the genial fat boy no more, and while he ridiculed others, he never laughed at himself. He could be mean as a snake, just because he felt like it. When the yearbook finally appeared that Pat and I had worked on hard and long, recruiting good writers like himself as contributors, I summoned up courage to ask him what he thought of it. "Not much," he replied. He meant to wound and he did, and I could have taken better warning from it, but I didn't.

When we necked in the front seat of his car in the Wash, we smoked and got high on beer or wine, and we kissed and felt various lumps, and then Paul would invariably put his head in my lap to be comforted. All the lit guys called their women "girlies" or "sex objects" to show how tough they were about romance, but Paul wanted a sex object much less than he wanted a mother. He would cry and cry, reliving his war the way my brother had in his malarial delirium, only now that the doors were open I felt desperately helpless, like a mother with a sick child. I stroked his hair and tried to soothe his misery and made it clear I would do anything for him.

Paul's family had a beach cottage at Balboa, so, knowing it would be empty, we drove down there from college one afternoon and got tanked on beer. We took off our clothes and lay down on the sofa, and it was easy for me to close my eyes and pretend to have passed out because I was certainly zonked. I felt him on top of me and thought, well, let happen what will. Only nothing happened. He fell asleep and so did I, and driving back to the campus, he said, "Boy, what I almost did to you and would have if you hadn't passed out." It was another warning, but I didn't want to be warned.

Paul graduated that spring and I continued straight on into summer school to be near him. At the family beach house, he was learning French to pass the language exams required by Harvard, where he would follow his brother in the fall. I was in Claremont, gulping down chunks of American literature as big as Melville's whale. I had already eaten Hawthorne and Emerson and Whitman and Thoreau and was finally learning, from a professor who was also a poet, how to digest modern poetry— John Crowe Ransom and Marianne Moore and Eliot and Pound. I was discovering irony, paradox, ambiguity. My writing was improving because I was beginning to understand what I read. I longed to talk about all of it with Paul.

But the action of love is rightly described as a fall. Balboa was only an hour and a half's drive from Claremont, but I waited by the telephone in my dorm for calls that never came. I had no car, and even if I had, women were not supposed to pursue men, at least not women like me who were trained to wait as we were trained to listen. We were like the chorus in a Greek play, responding like an echo to the actions of the protagonist. Once in Balboa, my protagonist found it more convenient to date his sister's friends.

One of his friends told me Paul was coming to Claremont on some errand having nothing to do with me and that he was going to have lunch in the Coop. I fixed and refixed my hair. I reshaved my armpits and polished the toenails that would show in my sandals and found a clean cotton sundress that tied in a bow on each shoulder. I rehearsed and re-rehearsed what I would say, how I would play it cool but warm, to show that I cared but didn't care. "Hi, Paul, how's it going?" "Hi, Paul, how've you been?" "Hi, Paul, good to see you again." "Hi, Paul . . ." If today I had to enact the emotion "Anguish" for some theatrical improv, I'd only need to imagine the mirror above the dresser in my room at Clark Hall and a girl with freckled shoulders watching herself mouth the words "Hi, Paul . . ."

I didn't see Paul again until we met by chance a year and a half later in New York. I had piled on courses so that I could graduate early, in January, and escape from the college walls that had once seemed so liberating. I intended only to drop my boxes of books and tattered clothes in Riverside, en route to Los Angeles or San Francisco to get a job. But Dad had to go into the hospital for yet another operation on his adhesions. He was so dispirited that tears came into his eyes as he squeezed my hand and said goodbye on his way into surgery. He made it through but he would be weeks recovering at home, and the D.O. insisted that I be there to help out. I was forced back into the bottle again, with the cap screwed tight and no openers in sight.

After a month, Dad was up and around and it was clear to me that my essential job was not cooking our feeble meals or washing the dishes or doing a once-a-week clean. I was there just to be there. They couldn't stand to let me go. Why can't you get a job in Riverside? they would ask. In publishing? I would reply. The truth is, I was unequipped to do anything, but publishing was a good excuse to leave. I spent my days between meals and dishes reading in my faded pink-and-blue bedroom, staying sane by reading *War and Peace* and *Anna Karenina* for starters, then on to the four volumes of *Remembrance of Things Past*.

When I went out at night on a date with a local boy, I smoked and drank to make up for all those hours lost during the day, then chewed Sen-Sens and opened all the car windows and put my hair out the window to get the smoke out. On Sundays, I drove to church and parked in back in the lot where we used to roller-skate, smoking cigarettes and listening to the radio, and returning when services let out to lie about the subject of the sermon. Mine was the misery of Sartre's *No Exit*, but it was partly self-imposed. I couldn't exit without my father's permission because I didn't want him to feel I'd run out on him. Every week I asked if I could go. The D.O. said it was up to Dad. Dad said nothing.

In April, I told him that some college friends had offered me a ride to San Francisco in their car, after the Pasadena wedding of a Pomona pal who happened to be from Riverside. I would stay with Pat's parents, who had moved north to San Mateo, until I could find a job and a boardinghouse in San Francisco. My bags were packed, they'd been packed for weeks, but not until the morning of the wedding did Dad relent and let me go.

He gave me his blessing in the form of a $25 war bond in my name, which I could cash in for $18.75. That was my dowry, plus a $500 debt to the college that I could pay off over time. On a scrap of paper among many such he'd scribbled on in the rest home where he spent so many years before he died, I found written in his hand—in pencil—"Bettie flew the coop and never came back." He'd misspelled my name.

In my brief time in San Francisco, I did indeed live in a boardinghouse on Pacific Avenue and stole enough bread and butter at breakfast to make sandwiches for lunch. By buying nothing but cable-car fare to get me to and from my job with a merchandising firm on Market Street, I saved enough money to buy a train ticket to New York, meant to be a temporary stop on my way, when I got money enough, to Europe. I spent three days and nights sitting up in the bar car of the Superchief, then changed trains and stations in Chicago. I spent the overnight trip to New York on the Twentieth Century Limited talking to a fellow I'd met in the bar car and so was awake to watch the November dawn light up the mists of the Hudson River and color its banks, past West Point, past the George Washington Bridge, before we dove underground to emerge in Pennsylvania Station. I'd burned all my bridges and smashed all my bottles. I had $20 in cash in my pocket and was on my own for good.

When I met up with Paul the following month at a party in the Village, I was living on Bedford Street, renting a pint-sized bedroom from a pink-chemised landlady who gave me stove privileges in a kitchen full of cockroaches, but no refrigerator privileges, so I kept my package of frankfurters on the fire escape and scraped off the mold before frying. Within the week I arrived, I'd nailed a job as file clerk in the production department of Alfred A. Knopf, where one of my tasks was to clean out dusty files of correspondence with writers like H. L.

Mencken, Kahlil Gibran, André Gide, Thomas Mann. What an idiot I was not to take home letters that bore their signatures beneath otherwise worthless natterings about production schedules and delayed deadlines.

I was scared to meet Paul again, but also curious about him and careful about what I wore. He was in his second year of graduate school at Harvard, having finally passed all three of his language requirements after failing Latin twice, which had put *him* in such Anguish that he had thought of jumping into the Charles, but it was winter and the river was solid with ice. We met in the basement kitchen of a town house on Leroy Street where artists and writers gathered to be fed by a wife who was a gifted and generous cook. One of our Pomona friends had rented a room there while he polished his short stories by day and took me to jazz joints by night.

After that, Paul wrote. I responded. From then on we corresponded. Paul said, "Let's." I said, "Let me think it over." I was very much alone. I wrote Pat in San Francisco, "What do you think? I know I love him but I'm not sure I like him." She wrote back tactfully, "He's got a strong personality, that's for sure, but if you think you can stand up to him, do it." I didn't know if I could stand up to him, but I knew I couldn't stand to live without him. I found that out after the apartment I'd been wanting for weeks finally became available. I took one look and my heart sank. The apartment now looked as dreary as the gray air shaft revealed through its lone window. I wrote Paul, "Yes, let's."

Invasion of
the Waring Blenders

I DIDN'T CARE A HOOT about the boxes of silver that arrived by the carload, Railway Express, containing objects I'd seen only in shopwindows. Thick platters, thin bonbon dishes, water pitchers, sugars and creamers, salt and pepper shakers, pickle dishes lined in glass, jam pots, bud vases, candlesticks, a dozen silver-rimmed glass ashtrays for individual place settings. In my family the good silver was silver plate. This bright new world stamped "sterling" had a romantic glow, but all I could think of was the work it would take to keep it polished. Besides, this loot was from people I'd never met and never would, people obligated to the parents of the groom.

Paul's mother had supplied me with a list of people she'd wanted invitations sent to—invitations I'd bought at great expense at Saks Fifth Avenue, engraved on cream-colored stock. I wanted to do the thing right. When I married Paul, I was marrying Pasadena, but fortunately none of Paul's mother's friends would know that we sold most of the silver to a secondhand shop in Boston as soon as the honeymoon was over. Pasadena

was three thousand miles away from Cambridge, Massachusetts, where we got married in Christ Church because of the
Revolutionary War bullet hole in its wooden door. I know that
history, tangible in a bullet hole, is one reason we'd both fled
California for the East. What I can't explain is why I've kept a
big box of the remaining silver all these years, unused and tarnished, like fossil relics from the Stone Age.

Besides the lode of silver, we also reaped a set of Revere
Ware, a pressure cooker, two copper chafing dishes, a toaster,
an electric waffle iron, a wooden salad bowl and matching individual bowls, a wooden salad serving set, a carving set, a coffee percolator, a copper teakettle, and—the only gifts we cared
about—not one but two Waring blenders. It was June 1949,
and the Waring blender celebrated not just the end of the war,
when technical ingenuity could once again be applied to the domestic front, but the end of Prohibition, for this was a machine
designed to mix drinks. While Prohibition may have ended in
1933 for some, for others of us the Eighteenth Amendment was
the Eleventh Commandment, engraved by the hand of God and
enforced by a local, totalitarian Moses. In my family, Grandpa
Harper. In Paul's family, Grandmother Fussell.

When I met Paul, Grandmother Fussell was a mere young
thing in her eighties. She'd been widowed for over fifty years,
soon after she and her husband came to Pasadena from
Philadelphia to improve his lungs. She bore two sons before he
died of tuberculosis, and she was left alone to raise them in
paths of righteousness. One escaped to become a journalist in
Seattle, the other stayed to become a corporate lawyer in Los
Angeles and to let his mother rule the roost of a distinctly Victorian henhouse. As a first-grade teacher, Grandmother Fussell
had taught generations of Pasadenans to read and write high

moral sentiments in verse, an art she practiced personally and explicated professionally as head of the local chapter of the Robert Browning Society. On the domestic front, her domain was the Sunday dinner table, where she terrorized her daughter-in-law and her brood each week after services at the Pasadena Presbyterian Church.

To terrorize Mother Fussell took some doing. Wilma was a short, square-jawed, black-browed woman with a quick sense of humor and an Irish temper to match. Her eyes were so deep blue they were black, and by the time I knew her she was as wide as she was high. We met her at the train station in Boston a week before the wedding, and when I saw this round pot roast of a woman with her hat stuck on square, puffing along the platform in her sensible shoes, I said to Paul, joking, "Hey, that must be your mother now." "That *is* my mother," he said, not joking at all.

When I first visited the family manse in Pasadena, Mother Fussell opened her linen cupboards, her china cupboards, her cabinets of glassware, her chests of silver, with the pleasure of a little girl showing off the furniture in her dollhouse. That's what mothers did. They bought things with the money given them by their husbands, who were always at the office and never home. They bought things for the house they spent all their time running, with the help of a hopelessly incompetent Lucinda, or Geneva, or Clarissa, and despite children who were always making a mess.

Mother Fussell was a fanatic cleaner and a good sewer, but a terrible cook. She was a carbo-loader who composed meals of mashed potatoes, buttered rolls, and macaroni and cheese to accompany the dried-out roasts and mushy vegetables, all of them penitential acts before the hallelujah of ice cream, cookies, and cake, all three rejoicing together, unless it was ice cream, cookies, and pie. While tobacco and alcohol were outlawed in every form, just as in my house, food of any kind was sanctioned as long as it was sweet. When her Paulie was a teenager, she stuffed him with candies and pastries until he too grew fat. Fat, he would stay home with her instead of chasing after footballs or girls.

Mother Fussell had put on weight at eighteen with her first baby, when her long black hair was still tied with a white bow, and she took off the bow but not the weight. Sixty years later she died of a diabetic heart attack, hating her oversize clothes, her sensible shoes, the body that had betrayed her with its addiction to foods that were her comfort. A year after she died, Father Fussell married a widow, a friend of them both, who was slim as a willow wand and wore pretty high-heeled pumps. In his rise to riches during the Depression, Father Fussell had outgrown his young bride, socially and intellectually. Her childlike forthrightness and emotional bluntness, often a source of comedy, could also have been a trial to a lawyer known for his discretion.

Paul was more like his mother than he knew, and he expected other women to be just like her, only smarter. When we announced our engagement in the spring, he gave me a drawerful of socks to darn and a number of buttonless shirts to mend. His first step in planning the wedding was to draw up a list of household equipment: 2 bath towels, 2 hand towels, 2 washcloths, 2 pair sheets, 3 blankets, 2 pillows, 1 bedspread. Marriage was about having a house and furnishing it.

Mother Fussell donated money for china and silver. We flouted her taste but not her aim, buying stoneware from Bonniers instead of flower-patterned Haviland from B. Altman's, and choosing handcrafted silver from Shreve, Crump and Low in Boston instead of a stamped national brand like Rogers. We took pride in our independence, but we didn't say to hell with all that and take off for Europe. Such a move was as unthinkable as to live together without getting married, which I'd suggested but Paul nixed. Only bohemians did that.

After the wedding, we'd held a small reception at the house of Paul's brother, Ed, who'd just finished his doctorate at Harvard before returning West. We'd decided to serve a temperance fruit punch for the sake of Mother Fussell, but Ed added a bottle of vodka for the sake of the rest of us. The day was unseasonably hot, and Mother Fussell drank glass after glass of "this delicious punch" and flirted with the minister until she sat on her glasses and squashed them and had to be helped back to her hotel. It was in this state that Paul was finally able to persuade her not to accompany us on our honeymoon.

If you could be almost virgins, any more than you could be almost pregnant, we were. Although we'd tentatively explored each other's bodies during the months before our marriage when we spent a few furtive weekends in hotels in New York or Boston, perjuring ourselves when we signed the register as man and wife, our shared emotion had been terror that the house dick would knock down the hotel door and expose us. Sex out of wedlock was a crime in Irish Catholic Massachusetts. So was sex within wedlock if procreation was not the aim. In Massachusetts, even condoms were illegal. In New York, venery was more venal, and by convincing a doctor I was about to get married, I got fitted for a diaphragm. The diaphragm, like the Waring blender, was an apparatus with talismanic power because it seemed not just to redeem the forbidden but to wallow in it.

Paul was as inexperienced as I, vet though he was. While his platoon mates had frequented brothels in Strasbourg and Paris, he'd read Henry James. We hid our ignorance behind nicknames and cleverness and literature. In our love letters, Phil Phallus wept tears of longing for Vera Vulva and, summoning Shakespeare, wanted "a hole to put his lolly in." Paul was Nicor, the little water monster in England's epic *Beowulf*. I was Nanny, the heroine of English nursery rhymes, whose sole function was to comfort Nicor.

Our honeymoon is forever associated for me with water monsters of another kind. We'd rented for the summer a cottage on Cape Cod. It sat by itself on a point of land surrounded on two sides by tidal waters that cut their way through a splendid beach in their rush to the sea. Our eager real estate agent had assured us that we could step out our front door and take a swim at will. She failed to mention that the water was chockablock with weird creatures we'd never seen before. They looked like frying pans with tails for handles, and they scuttled back and forth silently but with speed, looking to mount a mate. To step into the water was to risk being surrounded by horseshoe crabs, diligently copulating.

That's what we were doing inside, discovering each other's bodies in an orgy of exploration. I fingered the scarred indentations on Paul's back and leg where the mortar had hit. I couldn't get over how smooth his chest was, how hairy his legs. "Let me look at you," he'd say, telling me how beautiful I was, even as I kept trying to cover myself with a sheet. We numbered each other's moles and warts, ribs and vertebrae—we were both very thin—surprised at our sameness as well as our differences, and making a game of our fears. We played all day and all night and all next day, until guests began to come. Friends, professors, acquaintances dropped by, anyone we'd ever known and lots we'd never seen before, since we'd been fool enough to mention that we had a large number of beds in our honeymoon cottage by the sea.

Fortunately, some of these people introduced me to yet another water monster. I was skeptical about eating lobsters, which seemed to me as grotesquely armed as a horseshoe crab, but I was assured that the crustacean concealed meat while the arthropod did not. One of our college pals, who'd been East longer than we, demonstrated by filling a large tin wash bucket with water and laying in a bed of seaweed. He was a war vet who'd been through Iwo Jima and knew how to distinguish man from beast, and how to kill either, when necessary. He popped some lobsters in the pot, clapped a lid on top, and held it down with both hands as they bucked and reared in a vain attempt to escape. He cracked open a red claw for me and extracted in one piece the tender flesh with vestigial thumb, exactly the shape of its carapace. The buttery, delicate succulence of that flesh, and the hurdle of getting at it, was as erotic to me as any porn flick.

In those days no one thought of saving shells for stock. We filled garbage bags with lobster carcasses and took them to the city dump for the gulls to clean up. That's before I'd learned either to cook or to plan ahead. We were living gloriously, day by day, in the moment. One of my friends, a poet who was also honeymooning with her groom and had dropped in to stay a while, summed up the moment on a night when we'd all gone skinny-dipping in the moonlit waves and were trying to find our clothes. She was a large girl and she sat down naked on the sand with wet black seaweed hair. "I ope my legs to the sea," she said, opening her arms and legs wide enough to take in all the lobsters and horseshoe crabs, not to mention the clams and mussels and oysters and flounder and haddock and cod in the whole Atlantic and in all the earth's seas.

For a moment, we belonged to the elements. The rest of the time, Paul studied for his orals. By the end of the summer, he had to read and absorb all the works listed in chronological order in a booklet that staggered me in its scope—all of English language and literature, from Anglo-Saxon dental fricatives to Edwardian galloping dactyls (anything more recent didn't count as literature because it hadn't stood the test of time). Orals were a source of genuine terror among graduate students. A close friend of Paul's had failed and, in disgrace, was studying to try them again.

Just what I was supposed to do while Paul studied was unclear. If the Victorian America we'd both grown up in and not yet out of had defined our feelings about sex, the war had solidified our feelings about gender, a word none of us used. We spoke of men and women, not of male and female. A woman's job was to take care of her man. Somehow I hadn't counted on just how categorical were the imperatives of marriage, but I soon found out.

The flash point was a salad dressing. Salad dressings that you made yourself instead of shaking them out of a bottle were a big deal then. So were salads made of any other lettuce than wedges of iceberg green. Most of us didn't know there *were* other kinds. But I'd learned to make salad dressing in the blender, and one day on our honeymoon, on impulse I threw some salted peanuts into the oil and vinegar whirring in the machine. Although this was long before I'd ever heard of an Indonesian saté, I figured peanuts would make a good thickener. Paul was outraged.

"You don't put peanuts in salad dressing."

"Why not?"

"Salad dressing is one thing, peanuts are another."

Again I was warned. I'd married a pigeonholer and a basic pair of pigeonholes became the ground of our running argument for the next thirty years: men were one thing, women another. Their positions in the Great Chain of Being had been fixed by God for all eternity. Read Milton, for chrissake. "He for God only, she for God in him." No Waring blender, or any other modern technological advance, was going to join together what God had put asunder.

In Boston, the blender sat enthroned in the kitchen of our apartment in a tenement on Huntington Avenue. Our landlord was in prison, along with ex-Mayor Curley, for having attempted to burn down our building for the fire insurance. Drunks slept in the stairwell, and we sometimes had to climb over them to get to our door. Our own sleep was often disrupted by screams and the crash of shattering glass in neighboring tenements. The previous occupants of our apartment had painted all the walls and ceilings black, which we thought sophisticated, so we painted the odd pieces of cheap furniture we'd collected the same color, highlighting the stacked pine boxes we'd made into bookcases by painting them Harvard crimson. We were trying hard to be modern, just as I was trying hard to learn to cook some fodder more interesting to my new husband than hot dogs and bacon and eggs. The GI Bill was paying for his graduate school and we had a very small budget for food. But to make a thrifty casserole, to make your way around a kitchen, you had to know something more than how to open a bottle or can.

I'd known all along that my job at Knopf was temporary, although my boss had wanted to train me in the art of book production. He'd been disappointed and a little angry when I called him from a phone booth in the Whaler's Bar on Lexington Avenue and told him I was taking the afternoon off because I'd just got engaged. But Paul knew, and I knew, that the husband's job was to make money and to pay for the food, clothing, and shelter of the One Who Didn't. The wife's job was to prepare the food, mend the clothing, and tidy up the house of the One Who Did. Other duties of a housewife were to be pretty but not recklessly beautiful, to be attentive but never boring, to be intelligent but not to have a mind of her own, to be entertaining but never to upstage her husband, to be educated but for no practical or professional purpose, to be available for sex when wanted but not to want it on her own.

In comparison to the scrubby jobs I'd had before, this one seemed made in heaven. True, I was paid nothing, but after all, I hated to clean, didn't know how to cook, and was learning sex by on-the-job training, so you could say I was no bargain. At last I could learn to be a Lady and to have Nice Things— Mary Pickford's words when she began to make money in the movies after having worked the vaudeville stages of Canada and America since age five. To be released from the daily scramble of earning pennies to buy peanut butter sandwiches and moldy hot dogs, from the continual restitching of worn-out garments because you never had money to buy new, from the chronic headache of debts you could never repay, from the petty thrift of always taking a subway and never a taxi, from the automatic reflex of finding on a menu the cheapest dish, this was liberation. And I thanked God and Paul for it.

I'd been given a loose-leaf notebook of recipes as a wedding present from the wife of one of Paul's friends, an ex-Marine major. She'd typed them up in down-to-earth prose, as if telling

me over a kitchen table how to get by until I had time to work
out things for myself. It was as good a present as the blender.
Her Simple Macaroni and Cheese fueled countless fifteen-hour
days of study, once I'd weaned Paul from canned Franco-
American spaghetti. I learned to make her Spaghetti Sauce from
Scratch, with tomato paste and canned tomatoes and one clove
of garlic (left whole and removed later), along with cinnamon,
cloves, and celery seed. I learned to assemble the ingredients for
Tuna Casserole with Lipton's Onion Soup. Lipton assisted
many items in our menu, especially the ubiquitous and always
praised Clam Dip served with Ritz crackers. Dips themselves
were strictly postwar and a welcome sign that cocktails would
be served.

Our first cocktail party in the black hole was also my
coming-out party with Paul's fellow graduate students, most of
them married and most of them Ed's friends first. We decided to
serve sherry to simplify things. Besides, you could get high on
sherry fast. In addition to Clam Dip, we put on the dog with
Hellfire Cheese, cream cheese spiked daringly with mustard,
Worcestershire, and Tabasco. I'd bought a bright blue satin
cocktail dress for the occasion. I launched myself into the
crowded waters, promptly spilling a large glass of sherry down
my front. Unfortunately the satin was too cheap to survive the
baptism. The fabric didn't quite dissolve, but it came out a different shade of blue as it dried, like the sleeve that had once disappeared into Paul's mouth as a baby when his mother was
cutting out a dress to sew. It was a story she told well, how she
searched for the sleeve in vain until she spied a sliver of fabric
in the corner of little Paulie's mouth and drew out, like a magi-
cian from his hat, an entire sleeve of rose chiffon. People wondered, when she wore her new dress, why one sleeve was rose
and one was palest pink.

But learning to cook or play hostess was the least of what I wanted to do. Yes, I wanted to be a lady, but not a lady of leisure. I had a mind and the beginnings of a well-trained one, and why had I gone to college if not to gain knowledge of something more important than stoves? Paul had converted me all too successfully to the seriousness of humane letters, but I'd only begun to study seriously. Through him I saw daily how stupid I was. I decided to take a master's degree at Radcliffe while Paul took his orals and wrote his thesis.

I couldn't pay the tuition without help from Paul's parents. Father Fussell was always my ally. He knew I had brains and he enjoyed them. It was Mother F. who had problems with me. I was too much like her sons, whose learning had far outstripped her own. Later, in her sixties, she went back to college and drove everybody crazy when she fell in love with her TV-actor Shakespeare teacher and couldn't stop raving about him. But now she asked me, "What do you want an M.A. for?" My function was to breed as soon as Paul graduated. I used the excuse that even when we had children, once they were old enough I would want a job, and I would need an M.A. to teach.

Paul was mixed in his feelings about what I should and shouldn't do because he mistook education for intelligence. He actively hated his mother "for being so dumb," without perceiving that she was plenty smart, she just didn't have his or his brother's or his father's education. He was establishing his own world of absolutes and the relatives of social history were irrelevant. He demanded a mate smart enough and educated enough to understand his discourse, but he also demanded, Victorian that he was, subservience. He believed in the natural inferiority of women and felt that his mother fully substantiated that faith. So why hadn't he married a woman like her, I asked him in one of our ongoing arguments about the sexes. He could never marry a woman like that, he replied. Who would he have to talk to?

I knew it would be better for both of us if I went in for art history, but I'd have to start from scratch, with a slew of undergraduate courses. English it would have to be, but I hoped that as long as I stayed three steps behind, like a Chinese wife, I wouldn't crowd him. I was also careful to keep focused on drama, which to him was a vulgar and inferior genre. Shakespeare's poetry by definition rose above drama, as the printed Folio rose above the rabble at the Globe. Even so, when I started to write some plays of my own on my portable Corona, he said, "What do you know about dialogue, stagecraft, plot? What makes you think you can just sit down and write a play?" Nothing made me think so, nothing but the wish, so I stopped. I tried to find some local theater to join, but I didn't know amateur groups in Boston or Cambridge, and the Brattle Theater Company, which occasionally picked up undergraduates for its choruses, was a galaxy above anything I'd ever done or seen. In fact, the Brattle, with its company of Harvard vets, was so brilliant that Paul made it an exception to his general rule that Shakespeare should be read and not played.

While Paul spent every day in his library carrel studying for the dreaded orals, I spent every day in the black hole learning German and Latin with the help of Paul's boxes of word cards. I had to learn in a year enough to pass the triple-headed language exam that had driven Paul to the brink of the Charles. German was doing the same for me, with its Gothic lettering and barbaric syntax. But Latin was a language I'd wanted to learn since junior high, when my parents decided against it because I was working too hard without it and they feared for my health. The logic of Latin appealed to me, and I memorized vocabulary by sounding words aloud for hours on end, until the black hole began to close in, and I started to hear voices coming through the walls.

I entered Radcliffe with trepidation and determination. Boston and Cambridge still belonged to the Brahmin, and I looked with a Scots dissenting eye on that Establishment as on others. I seemed to be constantly violating unwritten rules of behavior, like wearing sandals on campus or saying "Hi" to my professors with a cheery California smile. I was a yokel again, twice over, a hick from Riverside and a hayseed from the West who nearly froze my toes in Boston snow before I traded in my sandals for boots. But as I walked into the green oasis of the Yard and up the library steps and into the high-ceilinged silent reading room and through floor after floor of open stacks, I felt lucky to be alive in such a place at such a time.

Worlds that I had barely glimpsed opened like sea anemones, worlds that had been fully formed and stabilized centuries before pioneers discovered gold in California. No war had ever intruded here, or so it seemed, to disturb the quiet pursuit of scholars tracing the loss of the umlaut in Anglo-Saxon or the rise of the octosyllabic couplet in Chaucer. Everything looked so old, the trees, the buildings, the people. I had longed for history and here it was, bound into leather-covered volumes, expounded in classrooms, visible in the bottle-glass windows on Boston Common, weighting the very air of Louisburg Square.

Schoolwork wiped every other slate clean. Truman had sent U.S. troops to fight in Korea, and even though I was strongly pacifist after the war we'd just got through, I had no time or energy to protest. Besides, we thought Truman a bumpkin and Bess a joke and politics in general a waste of time. And after I got my first grad school paper back, I had more pressing things on my mind. I had to learn to write all over again, and fast. Paul had no patience to help. He was a skilled essayist and had got through it on his own, and I would have to do the same. After glancing at my draft of a paper on Spenser's imagery, he said, "If I ever find out that you know as little about literature as you know about painting, God help you." He also pointed out that I had misspelled *Faerie Queene* throughout. In grad school a B was the equivalent of an F, and how I labored for those A's. I couldn't sleep before exams and couldn't eat breakfast because of dry heaves. Before the year was up my stomach was in such knots I was sure I'd acquired an ulcer.

And yet it was probably the single most exhilarating year of my life. Despite Paul's admonition *nil admirari*, I was full of wonder at my professors, whose apprehension was so godlike but whose persons were so weirdly eccentric. The hands of Harry Levin, as he expounded Renaissance and Jacobean drama, trembled so violently he could scarcely turn his three-by-five lecture cards. Douglas Bush, explicating the sources of Renaissance Humanism, was so shy that when he tucked his head into his chest to recite from memory not only Spenser's *Epithalamion* but all of its Greek and Latin progenitors, you could scarcely hear him. As Walter Jackson Bate illuminated the elegance of Pope, he would often extend a long arm over his head to dig in a nostril on the far side of his nose.

The pantheon of Cambridge gods—Alfred North Whitehead, Henry Wadsworth Longfellow, Ralph Waldo Emerson, George Lyman Kittredge, James Russell Lowell, William Cullen Bryant—was regularly evoked, George Santayana the only name falling short of a three-gun salute, but what could you expect of a Spaniard? To feel the breath of such Tradition humbled you in your successes, sustained you in your failures, and let you feel connected to something larger and more significant than yourself, the way the Church once did. Tradition could make your small individual life meaningful, and former Harvardian T. S. Eliot's "Tradition and the Individual Talent" was our credo. We knew *The Waste Land* by heart, and Eliot's Anglophilic conservatism in literature, politics, and religion had shaped our own. The night he came to lecture, Memorial Hall was jammed to the rafters hours before he was scheduled to speak and, once he'd started, crowds of students who'd been shut out shouted and pounded on the doors, like revolutionary rabble at the Bastille. It felt as if history was being made, and we were inside it, in a sure Place.

Paul pretended not to be worried about the orals, although he came down with an attack of the runs that went on for weeks. When he got the word that he'd passed, he telephoned me in a tone that implied "Natch." We celebrated with martinis at a local bar. Only later, much later, did he confess that he'd barely squeaked through because one professor had voted against him for not answering a single one of his questions. Where did Matthew Arnold as a child go to school? William Wordsworth? Samuel Coleridge? Samuel Butler? And on through the list of worthies. In a crisis, it was typical of Paul to pretend the opposite of what he felt. At our wedding, kneeling before the minister, his body shook so hard I put my hand out to steady him. Afterward, he claimed the service had been a breeze and a bore. His favorite word then, and for a long time, was "boring."

He wrote his thesis in a year, which was quick work for Harvard. We studied seven days a week. On Saturday nights we drank three or four martinis at a good bar, like the one in the

Copley Plaza Hotel, then ate cheap Italian or Chinese and ended up in a neighborhood joint that served beer in pitchers at wooden tables while a country-and-western group twanged. They reminded us that we were Westerners beneath our button-down collars and gray flannels.

Nonetheless, we weren't in a hurry to head back West. Paul's brother had gone to teach at Berkeley but was one of the handful who refused to sign the loyalty oath inspired by McCarthy's rabid anticommunism. The moral and political battles this caused in the Fussell family, added to the hopelessness of my own, kept us East. Paul took a job at Connecticut College for Women, in New London. The town was a mix of grand houses of the sort Eugene O'Neill had lived in when his father got rich and low-down saloons of the sort he'd haunted when he wanted to get drunk. It was the kind of port town where women who walked the streets at night were arrested for "lascivious carriage" and where babies occasionally were eaten in their cribs when the port suffered an influx of rats. The college was isolated from all this on a bluff high above the river Thames, the "th" pronounced, American style, as in "thanks."

We were given half of the second floor of a two-story house that had been converted into cubbyholes for faculty, within walking distance of the college. The kitchen at the rear had a fold-down shelf that doubled as a kitchen table and had to be folded up in order to open the oven door. The living room doubled as dining room and the bedroom doubled as study, with two desks side by side, acquired when the English Department found itself shorthanded and hired me to teach half-time. My title was Assistant in Instruction, for which I was paid $800. Paul's title was Instructor, for which he was paid $2,700. The academic hierarchy was as rigid as the Army's, and faculty

wives were treated as camp followers, even while they were ex-
ploited as cheap labor.

When a young Instructor revised his thesis for publication,
his wife, as was the custom, typed it in triplicate, proofreading
the manuscript aloud, antiphonally with her husband, line by
line, bracket by bracket, semicolon by semicolon, and crum-
pling up the carbons and starting over with each mistake. A
wife was meant to be a helpmeet, and in the academy the first
duty of a faculty wife was to do the onerous secretarial and ed-
itorial chores that were beneath her husband's notice. Her second duty was to appear, well groomed, on the arm of her
husband at all faculty social occasions and at the annual post-
Christmas slave mart of the Modern Language Association,
where, by giving evidence of his taste and intelligence, she
might increase his hirability.

These were the smiling Eisenhower years, in which Ike ran
the country and Mamie turned the lamb chops with the same
nauseous cheer. His blandness, her bangs were class-coded, and
we scorned the class. Yet the codes of dress and behavior that
governed institutions of higher learning in those years were as
strict as military ones. We once learned that a candidate for a
job as an English professor had been turned down because a
member of the hiring committee had observed that his finger-
nails were dirty.

What was curious about these caste codes was that this was
a women's college, with a woman president and a mostly female faculty. But these women had done their graduate work
before the war, at Oxford or Tübingen or the Sorbonne, and
had chosen monastic service over marriage and the family, ded-
icating the rest of their lives to elevating the one over the other.
No American university would hire them, certainly none of the

Eastern Ivy chain, so they turned their women's colleges into
secular monasteries where they hoped to initiate a few—very
few, because few were worthy—acolytes into the sisterhood.

They were brilliant women whose scholarship was as formi-
dable as their intelligence: Rosemond Tuve, the explicator of
Renaissance allegory and symbol; Dorothy Bethurum, the me-
dievalist and Shakespearean; Pauline Aiken, the Blake scholar.
They gave Paul a hard time, because he was male and "pro-
fessed" to be an academic. A man had to prove his worth triply
with this gang, who treated the latest young novitiate from
Harvard or Yale (they never stooped as low as Princeton) to a
dose of what Pentheus got among the Maenads. They dangled
the bait of promotion over the head of their victim while they
tore his work apart, whether that of the budding novelist
Richard Stern or the young poet John Hollander or the essayist-
to-be Paul Fussell, all of whom passed through their hands. I
learned not to be surprised at how fiercely these women identified with American soldiers fighting in Korea and how sorry
they were not to be in combat themselves.

I had never seen their like. I was in awe of their learning
even as I chafed at being relegated to Pot Girl, no matter what
my actual tasks. I worshipped at the feet of Roz Tuve especially,
and was constantly hurt that I mattered as little to her as the
box of fresh raspberries and the bowl of cream I left in homage
at her door, across the street from ours.

And yet, these women of high standards and high intelligence were also high-spirited and sociable and lovably human
once the cassocks were put aside. To our wee apartment they
came one New Year's Eve to drink French 75s of cheap brandy
and cheaper champagne and to play Sardines. We turned out
the lights and, like braille readers, felt our way through the

darkness. We touched Pauline first, half stuffed beneath the sofa. Roz, whom we stumbled over crouching in a closet, let out her usual North Dakota whoop upon discovery. But our boss lady, Department chairman Dorothy, had utterly disappeared. We searched in vain and she might lie undiscovered still, had not a hiccup given her away, squashed flat between the box springs and the mattress of our double bed.

These were women from whom I learned by osmosis what I'd begun to learn by lecture at graduate school. My mind was still like the empty bowl of the blender, begging to be filled, and what ingredients were to be had! From Roz, metaphor as a mode of perception, a way of knowing. From Dorothy, Shakespeare's insight into human character. From Pauline, Blake's creation of an entire water-colored cosmos. From others, because I could audit courses free, I discovered Virgil and Catullus. Under Suzanne Langer, I explored semantics and aesthetics and the roots of symbol and art. From an ad hoc team of historian-philosophers, I dug into the history of Christian thought from Augustine to Tillich. I had two years of intellectual bliss, in which I sopped up indiscriminately every drop that spilled from those overflowing brains.

Paul and I had been married five years by now and the constant question on all lips, from our parents to our colleagues, was: "When are you going to have children?" Neither of us had been ready when we married, at twenty-one and twenty-five. We weren't ready now, but for a woman to have children after the age of thirty was to risk deformities and moonfaced idiots. Every doctor told us so.

Once we'd made up our minds to it, we had trouble conceiving. Someone suggested we take a vacation. We decided to follow the coastline north all the way to Quebec in our little yellow Volkswagen, the purchase of which had outraged our

Jewish friends. The night before we were to go, a terrific hurricane hit the coast of Connecticut. Electricity was out, water was off, trees were down everywhere, but none had hit our car parked on the street. So in we hopped and followed the hurricane's path north through Rhode Island, Massachusetts, and on into Maine. As California transplants, we'd endured our share of earthquake jokes and it was rather comforting to find that the East, too, had its faults. Our baby must have been conceived in a deserted motel just this side of the Canadian border. I liked the romance of starting new life after a high wind in Bangor.

Pregnancy was lovely, because while my womb was filling my mind was already so full. We were lucky to have at New London Hospital an obstetrician who had transposed the revolutionary Lamaze method into American lingo and medical practice. He was my doctor, and because he had written a book on the subject, I soon became adept in the exercises of strengthening and relaxing, of training the mind to listen to the body. That was the only work I read on the baby to come. I was too busy translating the *Aeneid* and writing an article on *Four Quartets* and, during a paradisal week in a snowbound inn at Concord, Massachusetts, reading the collected works of Wallace Stevens. That was my preparation for motherhood. Paul's preparation for fatherhood was simply to deny that anything was happening at all.

Mother Fussell offered to come help with the baby the week following delivery, but we knew that spelled disaster. Her last visit, when she'd slept on the couch in the living room and clucked that she certainly didn't want to be a bother while we graded endless papers side by side in the bedroom, had ended in an outburst of tears and temper before she packed her bags for California and vowed never to return. Paul and I vowed as fervently to our drinking companions that after the baby came nothing would change.

Our favorite colleagues in drink and gossip were an oddly suited couple, a Wordsworth scholar from Yale who'd married a much older Anglo-Saxon scholar from Harvard. We were so naive we didn't know he was an alcoholic, although he outlived his wife by many years after he went on the wagon and became no fun. We just thought he really enjoyed the excellent martinis with double olives he prepared for us at five o'clock sharp for what we called, after some Eliot poem, the lavender hour. Nobody then was the least bit worried about smoking and drinking during pregnancy. I simply stopped both around the fourth month because neither tasted good, and I was listening to my body, which said, "Forget it." This meant that the lavender hour got increasingly boring for me, as I stayed sober and the rest got drunk. But I was also curious to see how easy it was for others, and how hard for oneself, to recognize the slurred speech, wobbly knees, intensified hilarity or gloom, and incremental repetitions of being sloshed. I knew Paul had hit his limit when every other word was "bad, bad, bad." The words in between were "boring, boring, boring."

Paul was having drinks at the house of our martini chums when, having stayed home to rest, I went into labor. Since this was a first, we had no sense of timing. I called Paul and told him to come as soon as he could. The hospital was but a twenty-minute drive, but our baby was born within half an hour of my arrival, with an encouraging push from the doctor and intense euphoria on my part. Why didn't everybody have a baby? Why hadn't we done this before? Euphoria lasted the full five days of my hospital stay, where nurses came and went with this tiny wrinkled tomato that was all mouth and all demand. "Feed me!" I knew the Auden poem.

Although we named her Rosalind, from *As You Like It*, her nickname was immediate and permanent—Tucky, from the beginning of Joyce's *Portrait of the Artist*, where Baby Tuckoo comes down the path with Moocow. Poor darling Tucky, her parents lived in literature, not life, and the babies in literature were all taken care of by somebody else.

Ambushed by
Rack and Tong

WOMEN BORN INTO A WORLD of disposable bottles and diapers can look back on the kitchens of our mothers, with their steamers and diaper pails, the way we looked back on the quaint farm kitchens of our grandmothers, who to get a pound of butter had first to milk the cow. But if my grandmother wanted to know how to do something useful in the household, like treat communicable diseases, clean paint and hang paper, blue and starch linens, make rouge paste or powder, remove stains from animal fibers, or care for babies, she could go to a cookbook. By my time, cookbooks had eliminated the care and feeding of babies, along with those other useful instructions. Even though cooking and mothering went together, and even though you used the same method to can and preserve food for grown-ups as you did to sterilize glass bottles and their contents for babies, baby hungers were in one category, grown-up hungers in another.

Still, grown-up hungers notwithstanding, once you had babies, your kitchen became a bottle factory, cloudy with steam and jammed with apparatus. In a chapter on baby care in a 1908 book called *Household Discoveries*, the author had set the tone for the next fifty years of germ terror that descended on mothers like a mushroom cloud: "There's death in the dirty bottle."

Even if you were able to nurse, there were bottles of water and juice to sterilize in the big pot your grandmother would have packed with Mason jars. You also had to have a rack to hold the bottles upright so they didn't rattle around. Before you could fill the bottles, you had first to boil the water that went into them as formula or juice or just plain water. You had to thoroughly wash with a bottle brush and strong soap the interior of each bottle and turn each rubber nipple inside out to scrub it clean. Then you filled the bottles, filled the pot with cold water two-thirds of the way up the bottles, slapped on the lid, and boiled the works twenty minutes by the clock. You removed the lid and lifted out the bottles with a large pair of tongs, because you had to cool the bottles as quickly as possible in a bath of cool (not cold) water, hoping not to break the glass, in order to get them into the refrigerator pronto. Any delay risked the breeding of germs.

I suppose if I'd grown up canning and preserving food myself, instead of watching my father do it, I wouldn't have felt so bushwhacked by all the equipment needed to sterilize those ever-multiplying bottles for ever-multiplying babies. But nothing could have prepared us for just how unprepared we were for parenthood. So determined were we that a baby would change nothing that we hadn't even figured out where to put one. The first week Tucky slept in a blanket-lined drawer. The next week we moved her to a narrow wicker basket that we could squeeze between our desks and the bed.

Breast feeding was a natural sequel to natural childbirth,

and I was enchanted by the sensation of my breasts bursting with milk and a hungry mouth sucking at my nipples. But Tucky not only cried when she was hungry, she cried harder when she was fed. In fact, she coiled up tight as a steel spring and screamed before, during, and after feeding, and often in between. At night, our tiny bedroom amplified her shrieks and the shocking sound of Paul yelling, fortissimo, "Shut up!" After that, we squeezed a crib into the space between the oven and the kitchen shelf, so that one of us, at least, could pretend to sleep.

I tried hard to sustain the illusion that nothing had changed. I attempted to read newspapers and literary quarterlies with one hand while I propped Baby Tuckoo at her feeding station with the other, which may be why she would take only a few swallows before she resumed screaming. So I took her off the breast and guiltily put her on the bottle. She no longer cried during feedings, but she cried before and after, in a way that was as distressing as she was inconsolable. We sought recourse in literature, quoting Lear's "When we are born, we cry that we are come / To this great stage of fools." For a week or two the noise of the vacuum cleaner seemed to soothe the savage breast. But the only trick that really worked was to put Tucky in the car in her portable bassinet and take her for a drive.

Just colic, said our young pediatrician, recommending ground beef along with applesauce for the first solid food, and cow's milk instead of formula. But milk was suspect everywhere, because of all the atomic testing that had been going on. Who knew how much deadly and invisible cargo the clouds had dropped across how many meadows, or where? The only nourishment that seemed safe for a baby was food that had been factory-sterilized in jar or can, untouched by human hands.

When it came to the care and feeding of the young, a chasm as big as the war divided the generation of our parents from our own. Mother Fussell's dictum was: "You've got to let them know who's boss." When on a visit I made the mistake of leaving Tucky with her for a couple of hours, I returned to find a red-faced Mother Fussell and a screaming tomato in the baby bath. "She's just as stubborn as my firstborn was," said Mother Fussell. "Little Edward used to climb right up the curtains to get away from me." I knew better than to leave any baby alone with Mother Harper. I could see her fingering little Tucky's neck when she held her, and knew she longed for the chance to give it a good crack.

Dr. Spock was our ammunition against the totalitarianism of our parents. But Spock was only a book, after all, and the squirming, squalling creature in your arms kept you from a leisurely perusal of the index to find out if it was choking to death or having an epileptic fit or just trying to test your will. Anxiety is all I remember feeling for what seems like years at a time. My chronic nightmare was that I had left something at the supermarket and couldn't remember what. Oh my God, the baby.

The culture at large seemed almost as anxious as I was. Hysteria over nuclear fallout had led people to stock jars and cans and bottled water for themselves and their children, in basements and backyard air-raid shelters built to precise government specifications. The pretense of civil defense against the hydrogen bomb made me as cracking mad as Joe McCarthy did. Who were they kidding?

My Scots-dissenting blood boiled over when even the college succumbed to this idiocy. I happened to be on campus with Tucky one high noon, returning books to the library, when the sirens shrilled, signaling an air-raid drill. Instead of proceeding

as directed to the "shelter" in the library basement, I turned
and walked out the library doors against the heavy oncoming
tide and, as if in a retake of the scene of the baby carriage
bumping down the Odessa Steps in Eisenstein's great film, I
pushed my baby carriage down the slope of the long, long hill
in what seemed to be slow motion, knowing at every stubborn
and determined step what it was to be alone.

Our kitchen now doubled as nursery, the sink as baby bath, the
counters as changing table and prep space for all those bottles.
This made the care and feeding of baby and adult mouths difficult, so we were happy to move to a dilapidated 1840s farmhouse in rural New Jersey when Paul took a job at Rutgers.
Like other Americans in the postwar years, we were drawn to
the idea of a house in the country. If it was the pull of nostalgia
that built Mr. Blandings' Dream House, with us it was the pull
of history—the further back, the better.

Our new landlord was a New Brunswick dentist who wore
Bermuda shorts and black nylon socks with clocks up the side
when he visited us in his role as country squire. He had bought
the farmhouse and its clump of outbuildings with a barn and
extended shack for the sake of the land on which they sat in
once grand but now forlorn isolation, approached through an
alley of black walnut trees in which wild guinea fowl roosted at
night. The landlord cared nothing about the house and we
cared nothing about the dollar potential of the land. It was the
classical proportions and the history of the farmhouse that gave
us joy and made us eager to restore it to its former beauty. We
loved the symmetry of double parlors below, double bedrooms
above, each with a working fireplace. We made a deal with the
landlord to fix up the place in exchange for lower rent.

In the half floor off the landing, we converted a maid's room into a nursery for the baby and a narrow ironing room into a study for me. We converted the parlor that adjoined the kitchen into a study for Paul. The matching parlor on the other side was simply for show. We scrubbed and polished, stripped and patched, painted and papered. We hunted out reproduction eighteenth-century fabrics to match our historically accurate wallpapers. With the help of a knowledgeable friend, we'd scurried around the Connecticut countryside buying antique colonial furniture, cheap at the time, to fill up the house in the style to which it had once been accustomed. Within a few months we'd created a colonial American gem.

It was like expanding from a custard cup into a casserole. The kitchen alone was the size of our entire New London apartment. It had been thoroughly modernized by its previous owners, who had laid down a vinyl brick floor to match the original ballast brick of the large but unusable fireplace at the far end of the room. They had put in a central island with a sink and cupboards beneath, and still there was room for an old pine kitchen table with turned maple legs and the set of spindle-back chairs we'd patiently stripped and refinished, and a playpen and a little canvas swing that fit into the doorframe between the kitchen and the laundry room. Here we could swing Baby Tuckatoo when she woke up crying in the middle of the night. But who was to swing me when I woke up the same way?

The kitchen was meant to be the family room, only we weren't a family. We were a man carving out a career and a woman with a baby attached, separated by the door between study and kitchen. The door was an apt symbol of how we conceived and misconceived the boundaries between us. Paul kept the door closed. In his study, he was always working or reading, which came to the same thing. On Sundays he read *The New York Times* behind closed doors while Tucky and I played in the kitchen, she on the floor or in her playpen, banging pots and pans together, I at the kitchen table. That year I translated all of Horace's odes into English for the hell of it, for the pleasure of it, for the sake of sanity when the walls even in this great big beautiful house began to close in on me.

I couldn't understand why, now that we had all the space in the world, inside and out, I should feel so restless, so claustrophobic. The rooms had sash windows nearly ceiling to floor that looked out on trees and birds and grass and fields, which dawn rosied in the mornings and sunset reddened in the evenings. One morning at dawn the land was so beautiful and so beckoning that I ran out the front door in my nightgown and whirled around in the dewy grass like Isadora Duncan in her scarves until reality clocked in and I slunk back inside with wet feet. In such surroundings, how was it possible to be miserable? And yet I was.

From the day we brought Tucky home from the hospital, I had not slept a night through. I seemed always to be listening, listening to the man next to me snoring, to the cats meowing, to the baby crying. I envied Paul, who never lost a night's sleep. Were men born different, with a sleep gene inside their snore machine?

Paul would drive the yellow Beetle to college every morning and I would tuck Tucky into her baby carriage and bump along the dirt drive between the walnut trees, looking for the one neighbor a mile down the country road who had a baby just our size. Her mother was ten years younger than I and we had nothing in common but our babies, but other than crows we were the only things moving in this deserted stretch of fields, and we needed to talk diapers and formula and toilet training just to hear a grown-up voice. After her husband was killed in an airplane crash and she moved away, the only sounds that punctuated the long days were the mewling and puking of Tucky and our kitty cats, the squawk of the guinea hens, and once in a while a knock on the door from Ben.

Ben, an ancient farmer from Pennsylvania Dutch country, came with the house as caretaker. If anything went wrong with our sole source of water, the wooden tower listing between our house and his shack next door, Ben was to fix it. In theory. In practice, he spent his days in an alcoholic stupor, from which he occasionally roused himself to shoot off a round of buckshot at the guinea hens. When we found a large rat in the guest bedroom and were betrayed by the cowardice of our macho black cat, regrettably named Mouse, who arched his back like a paper clip and backed hissing out of the room, we foolishly summoned Ben. He came with his rifle, eager to shoot up the radiator behind which the rat had taken refuge. We talked him out of that and down the stairs and ended up wedging a towel under the bedroom door while we thought of other solutions. We needn't have bothered, because for the next three days and nights, we heard Rat gnawing his way though first one closet and then the next on his journey back down to his family quarters in the basement.

Paul was thriving professionally, and with his increased salary we could now give dinner parties that suited our love of theatrics. We set up the central island in our farm kitchen for lavish buffets, consisting of platters of cold meats and American cheeses, potato salads, macaroni salads, tomato aspics, pumpernickel and rye breads, cake-mix cakes with ready-mix gloopy frostings, or desserts like canned shredded pineapple

with walnuts and whipped cream. We served highballs or
sherry with oversized bowls of potato chips and pretzels before
dinner, when with a lot of work a merry fire blazed in parlor
and study.

But we missed our former friends. It was hard to become
close to colleagues who were scattered so widely among the
surrounding burbs and urbs, each absorbed in his nuclear
brood. We leaned heavily on single, eccentric friends of dubious
sexuality, who weren't into marriage or family and would talk
and argue far into the night.

To us, talk *was* argument, and a major form of entertainment. We'd been well trained in our grad school boot camps:
attack with a thesis, reconnoiter in defense, and regroup for a
counterattack. Roz Tuve would rap your knuckles if you tried
to engage her in small talk when she was waiting to pulverize
your opinion of Eliot's essay on the Metaphysical Poets. When
the competition wasn't as tough as Roz, I enjoyed such parlor
games, encouraged them, played them all the time with Paul.
We argued the contents and discontents of literature from the
first cup of coffee in the morning to the last highball at night.
We sharpened our teeth on each other's sloppy propositions or
absurd conclusions. But now there was no place to put all the
talk we talked, and no place to go with it either.

A group of faculty wives would get together in somebody's
house once a month for sherry parties, which meant the deci-
bels rose fast but not my spirits. We gossiped about the department, our husbands and their jobs, the latest stupidity of some
dean or other university bigwig. Serious talk was limited to
children and schools and houses. I was not a happy camper, but
what could I say? I didn't want to grow my own tomatoes or
bake my own bread or learn how to paper my own walls and

fix my own plumbing. I wanted to talk about Shakespeare's last plays, which I was studying now that I'd finished Horace. I took notes on the plays, I took notes on all the criticism, but what for? For the pleasure of pure knowledge, I would tell myself, the kind of knowledge in the pursuit of Truth that Roz Tuve had talked about.

I'd just had my first scholarly article published, on the Augustinian structure of Eliot's *Four Quartets*, in a journal of repute. I'd submitted it to lesser journals earlier under my full Christian name and had been turned down. I switched to my initials and was instantly accepted as B. H. Fussell, a nom de plume that would serve me well for the next thirty years—who could take seriously anyone named Betty? As chance would have it, Paul had an article in the same journal, on the same poet.

But there was no chance of my applying for even a subsidiary job at Rutgers, which had strict nepotism laws. The formidably intelligent wife of the department chairman, who was a ninny, had been granted dispensation to teach one course at Douglass, the sister college to male Rutgers, but it had taken her a decade to get it. There were no other teaching jobs in the New Brunswick area unless you wanted to teach in the public schools, and I was above that. I wanted Scholarship and Art, not nursemaiding.

Another pregnancy kept me at home in any case. My new doctor practiced in Princeton, where he'd been a football star for the Tigers. He was of the old school, but I was trying hard to persuade him to let me deliver naturally, sans anesthetic. For my insomnia he prescribed a glass of brandy before bed. But brandy made me wide awake and eager to ask people over to party. As the months went on and I grew more and more fatigued, I was beset by crying jags that wouldn't stop. Could you have postpartum blues, I wondered, a year after partum? I thought of my mother, and wondered whether I'd inherited the breakdown gene.

Matters got worse when a Slav from Camden and his juvenile delinquent son moved in with Ben. Fired from his job at an auto works and kicked out by his wife, the Slav knew nothing about farms, but he too had a back-to-the-land vision of freedom for him and his son—and his newly purchased horse, goats, and a brutish pit bull terrier I called Fang. Ever ready with a literary reference, we called father and son, after Faulkner, the Snopeses. For the Snopeses, to live free meant that their horse could gallop across our lawn, their goats could eat every leaf of our shrubbery in addition to the milk and eggs left by our milkman and the newspaper left by our paper boy, and their dog could gnash his fangs at our cats and any other small critters, like our baby. I complained to the Slav, to Ben, to the landlord, all in vain. This was a free country, wasn't it? Fences were for city yards, leashes for city dogs. Why didn't I keep my baby inside?

On a snowy eve when the highways were already thickly blanketed, I went into labor, quick and fast. This time I knew to hurry. Paul bundled me and Tucky into the car and made for Princeton, as hell-bent as snow allowed. By the time we got to the hospital, I felt the baby pushing at the gates. The nurses got me onto the delivery table and told me to hold back, the doctor was on his way. But the contractions were too strong, and within a minute of his arrival, the baby's head was in his hands. I remember asking, "Is it a boy or a girl?" just before a nurse clamped a mask over my protesting face.

When I came to, the doctor gave me the bad news. The baby

had been stillborn. It was perfectly formed, they could find nothing wrong, but they couldn't make it breathe. Boy or girl? I asked again. If it was a girl we'd decided to name her Cecilia, after Dryden's "Song for St. Cecilia's Day." It had been a girl. We declined a casket and gave permission for an autopsy, which revealed nothing. My doctor was shaken. I was given sleeping pills and hauled away to a hospital bed. Paul drove Tucky home in the snow, put her in her crib, and when he pulled back the covers to get into bed himself, found a dead mouse on the pillow.

When I woke the next morning, I didn't recognize myself in the mirror. My entire face was swollen. I asked the doctor what had happened. "You cried in your sleep," he said. For the next four days I was trapped in bed behind dark glasses while colleagues and friends dropped by on sympathy calls. I hated it, whether they were full of cheer or commiseration. I was not going to feel sorry for myself. To focus on something concrete, I decided to learn classical Greek from a grammar someone had given me.

I was doing word cards the day the doctor came in and I told him that I had a funny lump in my throat that made it hard to swallow. Before I knew it a smiling surgeon was there, asking me to swallow, feeling with his fingertips what I could now see was a lump just above and to the right of the clavicle. "It'll be gone before you know it," he said, ever smiling. "I'll make a little incision here, just below, and we'll shape it in a semicircle so that you can cover it with a string of pearls, or makeup." You didn't question doctors. They told you what they wanted you to know. Evidently something was wrong with my thyroid and at the very least they'd have to take a look. Nobody said the dread word *cancer*, and it wasn't until I spent the night before the operation talking to the East Indian woman in the bed next to me, who had just had a breast removed, that I realized I was in the cancer ward.

It wasn't cancer. It was a freak rupture of a blood vessel that had destroyed one lobe of my thyroid, but I still had the other lobe and there were thyroid pills you could take if needed. My voice was hoarse, my throat was sore, and my smiling surgeon had indeed left me with a permanent pink smile of my own, just below the clavicle. But I didn't mind at all staying on in the hospital and eating quarts of vanilla ice cream. Besides, in the hospital I could catch up on my sleep.

Paul had hired a German housekeeper to look after Tucky and the house while I was gone. She was to remain another week after I came home. I hugged Paul, kissed Tucky, and asked after the kittens our cat Tiggy had deposited in the clean diaper basket in the laundry room just before I'd gone off to the hospital. In some unexamined nook, I was relieved not to have brought home another baby of my own.

I was lying in bed upstairs when I heard fierce barking outside and saw Fang racing across the snowy lawn into the bushes. Paul reported, reluctantly, that Fang had just killed Tiggy and her entire litter. The timing was bad. I had kept control in the hospital, after a fashion, but now I rose like a waterspout in my nightgown and robe and ran out barefoot into the snow, the housekeeper raising her hands to stop me, crying, "*Nein, nein, Frau Fussell, nein, nein,*" like a cartoon *Hausfrau* in the Katzenjammer Kids. I confronted the Slav, who had got hold of his dog, and shook my fist in his face. "Killers," I croaked. "Murderers." His eyes narrowed and he backed away, without apology, muttering about the right of every boy to have a dog.

Et in Arcadia ego. I knew we'd have to go, even before we

were notified that Paul had won a Fulbright to Heidelberg for the forthcoming year. But I couldn't let the Snopeses think they had beaten us. I took them to small claims court on the charge of recklessly damaging property, which wasn't hard to prove, what with the depredations of lawn and eggs and shrubbery and kittens and cats. But it was justice I was after, in a world in which there was none, in which babies could be born dead and kittens killed. This time luck was on my side. Unknown to me, Ben and the Snopeses had gotten drunk and stolen somebody's antique carriage at a distant farm. They were trying to hitch their horse to it when the owner caught them. The judge fined them a goodly sum and they had to sell the horse to pay the fine. I don't suppose anybody would have bought the dog.

I knew I was not in good shape. I'd have to take action and get out of the goddamn house. I wrote a letter to the English Department at Princeton University to inquire about applying for graduate school. I've saved the return letter from the chairman to this day because it put my dilemma so neatly. "Until now Princeton has never had any female graduates or undergraduates. This may be our loss, but it is certainly our policy."

Next I tried for a job at Princeton University Press. The director wanted to know why I wanted to work, since I had a husband and a family and I'd have to commute. I confessed that I had just lost a baby and felt I must take my life in hand. He was polite but embarrassed and I knew I'd muffed it. In desperation I took a job as a copywriter at a local radio station. When I got there, I was handed sheafs of boilerplate commercials for Gorstein's Hardware and Jake's Garage to read live on the air and told to keep my mouth shut in between. The paycheck wasn't enough to cover the cost of Tucky's day care and I quit.

With Paul's promise to look after Tucky in the evenings, I

landed the part of Elizabeth Proctor in Arthur Miller's *The Crucible* with the Princeton Community Players. Since the McCarthy witchhunts had provoked the play, I admired it as serious dramaturgy, and for a while it worked wonders in restoring my soul. As the tight-lipped loyal Puritan wife, defending her husband even after he'd confessed his lust, I was good typecasting. I was uneasy about Elizabeth's confession to her husband, though, because I feared it applied to me: "It were a cold house I kept." One morning when I was crying at the breakfast table and Paul asked me what was wrong, I said, "I don't know, I don't know, just get out." "Don't say that," he replied. Until then I hadn't even known I could hurt him.

That summer, on our way to Germany, we spent a couple of months in London. Our basement apartment in Knightsbridge was so dark and damp that washed diapers hung on a line grew mold before they could dry. A wire-mesh box attached to the window substituted for a refrigerator, and even with the cold it was hard to keep milk from curdling. Tucky lived, British style, on bread and jam because there was so little else to eat. The country was still on short rations, and anything other than tea or beer and cold toast and bread sausages seemed a luxury. I spent hours in Kensington Park reading, while Tucky placed her doll in the stroller meant for her and pushed it round and round Round Pond. The best food was pub food, but to get to a pub we had to call Nannies Inc. They sent us genteel elderly ladies in rice powder and lavender gowns who wished to discuss Shakespeare's sonnets instead of what time Tucky should go to bed.

Living in a London that was still in ruins from having been

bombed, hearing Brits talk about who'd been killed in the Blitz, hearing Big Ben toll what even then felt like the death knell of an empire, made us apologetic for being American. We scorned America as we scorned Russia, the pair of them bullies engaged in a Cold War instituted by fanatics on both sides. With war's effects so ominously visible, how could we possibly drop a hydrogen bomb over Bikini? How could the Russians possibly invade Hungary with their tanks? And yet we did and they did, both in the same year. The Cold War felt to me like little boys playing little boys' games with matches in a kitchen full of gas.

We wanted to explore every inch of Europe, and we could, because it was cheap, and we had American dollars. We took the ferry to Calais and, in the smallest of dockside cafés, I had my first bite of real butter and real bread. The wonder of those simple flavors and textures—the sweet and the yeasty, the creamy and the crisp—formed the base that sustained the harmonies and countered the discords of our travels through France for the next twenty years in search of real food.

From Calais we drove across Belgium and the Netherlands to Arnhem and down the Rhine, through Cologne, Mainz, Frankfurt. By the time we got to Heidelberg, we had seen what two wars stretched over thirty years could do to a landscape and its people. In the early fifties Americans were so unpopular in Europe, particularly in provincial towns where communism dominated local politics, that we'd pretend to be Swedish or English or even German. Paul cringed in the presence of tourists from Iowa, with their loud twangs and big bellies and dripdry suits, and he would tell me to hide my camera lest we be mistaken for the tourists we were. Like some nationalist transsexual, he felt he'd been born an Englishman in an American's body. I felt American to the marrow of my Bible Belt bones.

Still, I didn't like being identified as the enemy, and we were, especially in Germany. So the moment we secured an apartment in Heidelberg for the year to come, we escaped to the Mediterranean, abandoning Tucky en route in a Swiss nursery school in Nyon. She had been sick with some kind of stomach upset on the drive down to Heidelberg, but a doctor at the school thought she seemed okay. We left her and drove off across the Alps, through a blizzard at Brenner Pass, and down into the sunshine of Italy's Adriatic coast to hop a ferry at Brindisi. We were free again.

In Greece we consumed centuries as if we'd never eaten before. Every day we could now taste and touch and smell what we'd stored up in our minds from books, enjoying the gap between the two—the fluted columns of the Parthenon pocked by air pollution, the garlic breath of short dark Greeks with dwarfish legs who looked not at all like Pericles' Apollo in marble.

We shipped across to Sicily, glad to pass safely between the points of land we knew only as Homer's Scylla and Charybdis. In a trattoria in Erice, while devouring our first *fritto misto*, we picked up an English sailor who ran the radio equipment on a Greek oil tanker and was off for a week to spend his "stash of lolly." He was an upper-class type who'd been sunk once too often on destroyers during the war and had opted out for good, content to read books on shipboard and train the falcons who landed on his radio antennae, one of which he sported on his arm, hooded in its leather cap.

We became a scapegrace trio, astonishing the natives in remote coastal villages not only with our hooded falcon but with our blue eyes and blond hair. Many had never seen a "foreigner," so it was not hard for us to pass ourselves off as a Hollywood film crew. We picked names that we thought might sound vaguely familiar or at least plausibly foreign—Elia Kazan for Tony, Troy Donahue for Paul, Veronica Lake for me. Tony would burst with his falcon into some dank eatery and call for champagne for the house and ask where he could buy film, and within minutes every man in the village was crowding around, all talking at once, while Tony jabbered in his fake Italian and Paul and I tried to keep dark hands from feeling us all over to see if we were real. We were and we weren't.

We dropped Tony in Palermo to return to his ship and drove to Nyon, where Tucky burst into tears when she saw us. She had been very sick with bronchitis and the school had been very anxious because they'd had no way to reach us. We were back in the Real World.

But the year in Germany turned out to be more like a paid vacation for me, because there was always someone to help look after the baby. We employed so many nice ladies who came for that purpose that Tucky rebelled: "Nice lady not come!" Europe was different from America; you weren't expected to do all your own work. If a mother was educated, she was not expected to be a full-time housekeeper, nanny, and cook. There was no question of my spending much time at the stove in any event, because the kitchen in the apartment we'd rented had but a pair of burners set on a table next to the sink and the bathtub. I could fry up a Wiener schnitzel and bathe Tucky at the same time.

I did have a miscarriage in Heidelberg and worried about it a bit, after the stillbirth. But I took it as only a momentary defeat, even a kind of triumph, because the doctor prescribed coffee and red wine, and in Germany both were excellent. And sure enough, before long I was pregnant again and full of appetite for German *Kartoffeln* and *Nudeln* and, above all, the big bowls of *Schlagsahne* that German ladies wolfed down for a midmorning snack, placing their Teutonic bottoms on stools before a counter to spoon up mountains of whipped cream.

Paul had been twenty when he'd fought as a lieutenant in the Army's 103rd Infantry Division in Alsace. He'd lost most of his rifle platoon to German mortar fire in the snowbound woods outside Nancy before he was wounded himself. It was unsettling for him to return as a civilian to the homeland of the enemy, especially when we were so often mistaken for part of the U.S. Army of Occupation. There was a large American Army base just outside Heidelberg, and Army uniforms crowded the narrow streets, jammed the *Bierstuben*, and thronged the castle on the hill. The Germans tended to regard the Americans as barbarians or, worse, as killers of innocent women and children. This was not for them the Good War. Even educated Germans were more likely to identify with English culture and to equate Yanks with brute savagery.

No one had been a Nazi, no one knew anything about concentration camps or about bombing London. Germans had not been aggressors but victims of an injustice that provoked rage and outrage in their hearts. We met only one German, in the Anglischiste Seminar of Heidelberg University, with whom we could talk directly about the war. Most of the professors had been too old to fight, had lost their positions under the Nazis, and had been sequestered where they could do no harm. Most of the current students were too young to remember anything but bombings and hunger and fear. But one young faculty member had been a soldier at sixteen on the Russian front, at Stalingrad, and could tell war stories with an irony that matched Paul's. It was Herr Iser who showed us the photographs he had taken of Russian hostages hung from the trees, silhouetted like skeletons against endless fields of snow. Paul and Wolfgang talked as soldiers while his wife and I drank coffee and talked about *Kinder, Küche, und Kirche*, even though she was finely trained in English and was at that moment translating into German a major American work of literary criticism.

Although Heidelberg had escaped severe damage to its picture-book bridges and castle perched high above the Neckar tal, signs of war were everywhere. You could read them in the beer halls of the dueling societies of prewar Heidelberg, where aristocrats had worn their scars as badges of honor. Upriver, Albert Speer's house stood empty as a reminder that the man who had once drunk Gewürztraminer in his garden was now in prison composing his memoirs of innocence. Downriver, the ruined town of Mannheim had risen from its ashes in a magnificent opera house, where *Parsifal* was performed on Helden Sontag and the audience sat silent for a full ten minutes after the curtain had dropped to honor the heroes who had died for the Fatherland.

We traveled everywhere we could, like people with a toothache, probing the aching cavity. We toured half-crumbled cities like Köln—the German name rang like a bell, whereas Cologne sounded like cheap perfume. We couldn't go to Dresden because it was in East Germany. We couldn't go to Berlin because of the blockade that preceded the Wall. We could go to Munich. In enormous underground beer halls where two or three hundred linked arms, their mouths full of *Weisswurst* and bock beer, to sing "Ich bin Edelweiss," it was not hard to imagine the young Socialists of 1933 singing up from the ashes of ruined Germany their new Parsifal.

Or we could cross the border into France to visit out-of-the-way sites like Oradour-sur-Glane, preserved like Pompeii as a

town of ashes. The war had altered permanently categories of
fair and unfair, soldier and civilian, and the six hundred and
forty-two dead of Oradour-sur-Glane were mute testimony to
that fact. The June I graduated from high school, a German soldier had been killed by the local Resistance, and the SS had entered the village in force, machine-gunned the men, herded
the women and children into the church and set it afire, then
torched the village. The houses went up like a box of *allumettes*
and the smell of burnt flesh hung in the woods for months.
What was so disturbing in the ruins was the particularity of the
houses and their incinerated contents, here the blackened remains of a stove, there the twisted framework of a treadle
sewing machine. Oradour showed the underside of heroic battle in the field, the messy reality of ordinary people slaughtered
in the middle of their everyday lives.

I had the same feeling when we visited Auschwitz in the
1970s. What struck me most was how the bunkers where Kom-
mandant Rudolf Höss had displayed his efficiency with Zyklon
B were right next to the backyard of his family house, where
Frau Höss had hung out the laundry on lines that were still in
place beneath the trees, and where she must have complained
to her husband from time to time about the smell and the soot
that besmirched her sheets. Here it was that little Fritz and
Heidi, or whatever their names, had played tag until she called
them in because Onkel Heinie was coming for tea, and Onkel
Heinie Himmler loved children. *Kinder, Küche, und Kirche*,
universal as death.

I was eight months pregnant by the time we returned to New
Brunswick on the *Flandre*, a small boat that rocked violently

when a hurricane overtook us, making me, for the first time and to my utter disgust, seasick. From Heidelberg, sight unseen, we had rented a modern cement slab of a house in a Rutgers enclave in Piscataway. As it turned out, we developed a penchant for slab houses and went on to live in two more. I might have taken heed of the words of one of the drunks in William Saroyan's *The Time of Your Life*—"No foundation, all down the line"—but I didn't.

With this birth, my doctor insisted on complete control. He put me in the hospital and induced labor the moment I began contractions. For the first time I experienced a labor that was slow and painful and, because he insisted on giving me gas, I was cheated of the explosive moment of birth that was like pushing out the globe of the earth in a geyser of water and glop. But none of that mattered, because here was a baby boy, pink as a little pig, named officially Martin after Martin Luther and unofficially Sam after Samuel Johnson. I said, "No more literary names, please." Paul said, "Luther was a writer but he wasn't as good as Johnson." But when our son was eighteen, he went down to the courthouse at Trenton and officially changed his name to Samuel. He was quite right. He had turned out to be a Sam and not at all a Martin.

Paul did night duty with Sam, who fortunately was a smiler rather than a screamer and easily placated with bottles of apple juice in between the milk. Unfortunately, there'd been an outbreak of impetigo in the hospital, and when his skin showed signs of it, I'd been ordered to give up nursing for fear of breast infection. It seemed such a waste of all that self-generated nutritious fluid that made me one with the cows and cats and gorillas and elephants. On the other hand, I was free to move around, so I went into New York once a week to take acting classes with Uta Hagen in the Village. I saw theater as a practical diversion, because it was something I could do at night that wouldn't interfere with daytime responsibilities, and I could do it with amateur community groups so that it couldn't be considered a profession or a real job or in any way a competitive threat. And since drama had always been my passion, I decided that if I was going to do it, even as an amateur, I should take some lessons and do it right.

I could have applied that same axiom to motherhood, but I didn't. I chafed at motherhood, as I chafed at keeping house, because housework, no matter how hard you went at it, didn't count. Having babies and vacuuming floors was what you did with your left hand while you got on with your real work. *Arbeit Macht Frei*. But what work would make me free? That remained the question as long as I stayed with Paul, and I couldn't find an answer because the more strongly the answer was felt, the more it had to remain unspoken. My real work, full-time, was to take care of Paul. Everything else was peripheral. Everything else, including children, came last.

Tucky was old enough for nursery school, so I would drive her there and hop a train to New York and take a subway down to my old stomping ground in the Village and climb up the stairs in the little studio on Bank Street and join the assortment of students, most of them a decade younger than I was, gathered there to hang on Hagen's every word. She was born to teach, and I was born to study, and I did my homework on improvs and Method exercises as intensively as I'd gone after Latin or Shakespeare. "Be a teakettle on the stove" was something I could do. "You're coming home late a little tipsy and you can't find your keys." That was also something I could do.

But what I liked most was learning what other people did,

how they revealed their real life through pretense. As did the young Chinese girl who was making a pretend omelette in her kitchen. I watched how she put on her pretend apron, how she broke each pretend egg and separated the white from the yolk by pouring the liquid between the two halves of the shell, and how she wiped her fingers clean on her apron after each egg. I'd never separated eggs that way nor worn an apron in the kitchen, I'd never thought of using an apron as a towel. What a good idea.

I liked the idea of creating a secret language of associations that could trigger particular emotions on demand. There was the voluptuous Italian girl who was to mime walking to the grocery store and who walked with discomfort and great embarrassment. "What was your association?" Hagen asked. "A tight red dress my mother gave me that I hated," the girl replied. Who would have thought?

The problem with this Method was that it led me to construct a parallel world of emotions and to connect them in a parallel plot. "You're at the breakfast table and you're angry." Okay, I'm at home in Riverside and the D.O. has just silenced me with a frown. Bank that image of a frown. "You're waiting for a train to take you to New York to meet your lover." I'm in the living room in New Brunswick and apprehensive because I anticipate Paul's frown. Wait a minute, Paul's frown is like the D.O.'s, in relation to me. What connects them? Whoops, that's a separate plot.

We were assigned scenes from plays and students to rehearse with. I rehearsed a scene from Osborne's *Look Back in Anger* in the fourth-floor walk-up of a man who was working in an ad agency until he got his lucky break. His apartment was very like the setting for the play. We were to do the scene where

Alison and Jimmy have a big fight in their studio flat while she's
doing his ironing and they end up making love on the floor. Hagen had taught us how to really get into it, how not to indicate
emotion but to generate real emotion from the inside out. Trig-
gering anger was easy for both of us. Expressing that anger by
grappling with each other and falling down on the floor got
easier as we went along. But the transition from fighting to
lovemaking was all too natural. I was flattered that my partner
wanted to extend the scene with me but refused. That would
ruin everything, like my permission to be there at all.

We began to give dinner parties in the slab house, enticing
the Princeton literary set up Route 27 with lavish displays of
food and drink. In Germany we'd made friends with a Fulbright couple who lived in Princeton and were part of a circle
that sat at the feet of R. P. Blackmur, a poet and critic who was
a maverick in the academy—no Ph.D.—and the smartest man
I've ever met. Like Dr. Johnson, he had absorbed a great deal of
the world's learning and expounded it best in conversation.
There was reason to sit at his feet and pay attention to his
words. Although he could be ruthlessly cruel, he was also a
sage, and I was flattered when he took a shine to Paul and me.
He invited us to join not only the elect at the invitation-only
Gauss Seminars, which sponsored guest lecturers of renown,
but also the super-elect for drinks at his house afterward. This
was a world I'd been missing at Rutgers, a world I wanted to
join. Paul's ticket of entrance was his own sharp wit and literary acumen. Mine was as a well-packaged and intelligent sex
object who gave good value as a hostess.

One night when Paul couldn't go to the Gauss, I went without him, and afterward went on to drinks at Blackmur's. It was
a heady crowd of writers and aesthetes and intellectuals, including Kingsley Amis, Al Alvarez, R. W. B. Lewis, Eric Kahler.

Paul had asked me to come home early because he wanted to make love. I said I'd try, but I got home late. Paul was angry. "We had a date," he said. To me it felt like blackmail. I felt a constant current of hostility from him and, for the first time, thought seriously of packing my bags, bundling up the children, and leaving. But I could already hear him asking, "Where would you go?" I certainly couldn't run home to Mother. Without a cent of my own, I certainly couldn't take off for New York or some other city and expect to land a job that would pay for an apartment and care for the kids. No, the thing to do was to have another child.

When I found I was bleeding all the time, between periods, I consulted my doctor, who said that an embryo was in the womb but wasn't properly attached, so no doubt it would abort within a month or so. But it hung in there and grew while the lining continued to bleed. It was inconvenient to wear Kotex all the time, but this fetus showed remarkable staying power and, after the fourth month, the doctor thought it had a good chance to come to term. By the sixth month I switched into my well-worn maternity clothes.

It was Christmastime and our whole family had been invited to a house party of about ten people on a farm in Massachusetts, the childhood home of one of our Princeton friends. We drove up on Christmas Eve through miles of snow, thicker the closer we got to Bedford, to spill into the warmth of the farm kitchen with its old-fashioned woodstove and a table heaped with Christmas goodies and six or seven dogs leaping up to lick us and good friends to greet us. We had a sumptuous meal, because the hostess was a splendid cook and the host kept running down to the wine cellar for one more dust-covered bottle of her father's claret.

I woke in the middle of the night with what I assumed was

indigestion from major overindulgence. But the pains went on and on. I lay awake until dawn, when the pains became rhythmic and I realized belatedly that I was in labor. I roused Paul, who roused our host, because there was a blizzard outside and our Beetle would never make it to the nearest hospital. I didn't have any slippers, so our host ran back into the house and got his own. It took us about an hour to get to the hospital. By now the pain was unlike anything I'd ever felt before, not rhythmic but a bonfire in my gut, burning my insides out.

I begged the nurses for something, anything, to ease the pain, but they said they could do nothing until the doctor arrived. Where was the doctor? Making his way through the blizzard from his farm, far too early on a Christmas morning. Like my father, I'm usually stoic about pain, and when the going gets tough I get silent. But this time I was screaming. It's the only time in my life I've thought death might be better than more of the same.

As soon as the doctor got there, he gave me a shot that knocked me out. When I came to, I'd been delivered of a six-month fetus, in pieces. Evidently the baby had died at least twenty-four hours earlier in the womb and was starting to decay.

But the weird thing was, my body was suffused with the same kind of euphoria as if the baby had been born well and whole. Joy of some kind must have shown in my face because Paul asked, "Have they told you?" And I said, "Yes," and kissed his hand because I loved him and our friends and our children and life. Even though I was exhausted from pain and knew we would have no more babies, I felt all the same strangely blessed to be alive to tell this winter's tale. Winter was a time for death. Paul had died, he once said, in the deep winter snows of the Vosges Mountains when the rest of his men had been killed, but he'd come back to life to tell the tale. I knew that the wounds of childbirth were nothing in comparison to a soldier's wounds, but still I felt a connection. It was Virgil's "the tears of things." Men suffered one way, women another. But to me there was a kind of peace in surrendering to the rhythms of winter snow and greening spring that quite overrode the deaths men die for honor and women for love.

Hot Grills

IT BEGAN INNOCENTLY ENOUGH, with family picnics, the way Camembert begins with a meadow full of cows. But that was a few years and hundreds of hot dogs later, long after Paul and I bought our first house, a cottage paneled in knotty pine and hidden among blue spruce on Queenston Place, just off Nassau Street in Princeton. It was a dollhouse that wouldn't have taken five minutes to burn to a cinder, and as long as I lived there I feared fire.

We picnickers were mostly young academics in our thirties, from Princeton and Rutgers, some with young children, some without, all of us frolicsome. R. P. Blackmur was our rubicund Lord of the Revels, our Bacchus, with vine leaves in his white hair. The respectables of the Princeton English Department scorned him as a mere writer, a poet-critic with no scholarly credentials at all. And of course they scorned anyone from Rutgers, a state university. But we saw ourselves as outsiders because we cared about Art, in contrast to the philistine Establishment.

Most of the men in our group had been in the service at
least briefly, and we all recognized combat as the dividing line
between innocence and knowledge, deferring to our vets as we
deferred to our sages. For we took combat as the norm, and
within the sure Place of the Establishment we fought a guerrilla
war as subversives.

Picnics in the wild were rebellion against the white-glove tea
parties given by graying deans and their mousy wives. We were
bursting with youth, ambition, and libido, and they were not.
Picnics were also a rebellion against the four-walled kitchen
lives of us faculty wives, bored with changing diapers, fixing
school lunches, arranging cocktail parties, typing our husbands'
manuscripts, shuttling our kiddies to ice hockey or ballet. A
picnic got you out of the house, away from the eternal routine
of setting the table, washing pots and pans, and making and
unmaking the marital bed, which, once it had served its procre-
ative function, left little time for play.

And we were desperate to play. We had cleaning ladies and
babysitters, but none of us had live-in help. Even if we could
have afforded it, a servant by any name would have violated
the do-it-yourself code that was a battle cry for us who led
kitchen lives. We had discovered, by God, that you didn't have
to buy cotton batting in the supermarket, you could make
bread from scratch at home. By God, you didn't have to pay a
dollar a jar for a smidgeon of baby food, you could make applesauce from scratch in your blender. By God, you didn't have
to break your budget by eating in a fancy restaurant where the
waiters sneered, you could create in your own kitchen a three-
star, five-course meal and have money left over for wine. Of
course it would take you two weeks of hard work to do it, but
as your husband might unkindly remind you, what else did you
have to do?

Curiously, our picnics were not a rebellion against kitchen work. The woman who cooked indoors cooked outdoors as well. I don't know if blue-collar men were grilling hot dogs and hamburgers in their backyards in the early sixties, but I do know that white-collar academics were not, any more than they were going bowling, hunting, or to the Elks. It was women who toted the bags of charcoal and loaded up the Weber grills and squirted kerosene and watched the flames explode and then subside and the gray ash grow while they manipulated six pounds of ground chuck into thick patties and laid out giant wooden bowls of chopped iceberg lettuce and tomatoes and grated red cabbage slathered with blue cheese dressing and shooed the kids away from the grill as they chased fire-flies and each other, while the men stood around and drank. Heavily.

Princeton was an outpost of Cheever territory, where you could drink your way across town from party to party in one long moveable feast. While the women tended the grill, the men tended the thermoses of iced martinis and wrestled with the corkscrews that opened the wine and dispensed the brandy and cigars that finished off the meal. Drinking was men's work, and the men went at it manfully. The women drank too, of course, and not just to keep up with the men. Drinking was vital to our picnics, loosening tongues and lips and hearts and kidneys. Men could turn their backs and pee openly in the bushes. Women had to choose their coverts more carefully. But the un-spoken rule was that you could do things on a picnic that you couldn't or wouldn't do in a parlor. Such license was sanctified by a host of pastoral forms, literary and cinematic: *A Midsummer Night's Dream, Smiles of a Summer Night, Women in Love, Daphnis and Chloë, Roman de la Rose, As You Like It,*

Les Règles du Jeu. Food and wine on a greensward or under a grape arbor or even in a backyard were by nature a provocation to lust. Or at least to serious flirtation.

These days we drank, when the cocktail thermos was drained, iced Chablis or an inexpensive Médoc in stemmed glasses. The men had begun to drop the names of wines as easily as the names of obscure Metaphysical Poets, but no matter what the quality of the vintage, the results were the same. Prescriptions for hangovers were as lengthy as the drinking that had caused them. The only thing that interrupted hangover talk was being hangover horny.

Actually, being horny was the reason for our picnics, drink merely the excuse. We had learned during wartime, first the hot and then the cold one, to seize the day. If the Jerries didn't get you, the atom bomb would. Today was it, and we wanted to gather all the rosebuds we could find, *now*. The night after we moved to Princeton, Paul and I hired a babysitter and drove to our first dinner party in nearby Kingston. The party was still booming at 1 a.m. when our sitter's mother called, reminding us quite firmly that we'd promised to be back by midnight. Rather than break up the party, we simply shifted it to our house, and at three in the morning we were swinging in the children's swings in the backyard and building castles in their sandbox and making far too much noise.

Sex was in the air and on our lips and in the pressure of our bodies when we kissed each other hello and goodbye, a social custom that had infiltrated America's upper bourgeoisie in the fifties and lingered on, putting a full-mouthed American twist on the Continental habit of kissing both cheeks in greeting. Women rubbed cheeks so as not to leave lipstick behind, but women and men rubbed bodies together like Boy Scouts start-

ing a fire, and the prolonged good-night kiss that began as ritual courtesy might end as rendezvous. Or not. It was an era
good for kissing and flirting without anything happening at all.

Except, of course, it did. It had to, the way the Cold War
eventually had to hot up after the prolonged foreplay of threats
and counterthreats, simulated and real. With Ike and Khrushchev flashing their missiles, Russia was bound to fire off a
Sputnik and a Lunik just as we were bound to counter with a
Jupiter and an Apollo. Nationally we believed we were in control of our fears, just as privately we believed we were in control of our lusts. Self-delusion clotted the air like sex, and it
took but a small charge to blow it sky-high.

Our Princeton pals had already been primed by a quartet
of Brits, writers and their wives, who'd revived the days just
after the war when a crew of bacchants had danced across
the quad—John Berryman, Delmore Schwartz, Randall Jarrell,
Allen Tate, Robert Lowell. But the Eisenhower years had lulled
the Establishment into a false sense of security, so when Lucky
Jim arrived at Princeton in the person of Kingsley Amis, few
were prepared. Kingsley cut a swath a mile wide through the
faculty wives, literally laying them low with his charm, celebrity, curly blond hair, and bad-boy antics. He'd propositioned
me once in the bathroom of our house in Piscataway while I
washed out baby Sam's diaper. "Not quite my idea of a romantic setting," I said. "Oh," he said, as if surprised, "would you
prefer a bed?"

The Amises had inspired a whole year of husband- and
wife-swapping in Princeton before we moved there, and I didn't
know whether to be sorry I'd missed it or glad. There was no
scandal left in who had slept with Kingsley. Who hadn't? The
Amises were so very English, and yet not at all like the English

revered by the English Department and mocked for all time by
Lucky Jim. I tried to imagine resisting Kingsley's irresistible
combination of comedy and sex, as he single-mindedly put one
in the service of the other, and I longed to be put to the test.
Laughter is the most powerful seduction of all, and for these
English, America, with her straitlaced Puritans, was one big
laugh-in. They would as soon fuck as say the word; they
seemed to have no verbal or sexual inhibitions at all.

In Princeton the Amises lived out scenes Kingsley had already written in *Lucky Jim*. They accidentally burned a bed-
sheet in their rented house and tried to cover it up by cutting a
hole in the sheet; Kingsley went off to Yale to deliver a lecture
and forgot his briefcase with his speech inside. They were also
living out scenes that would appear shortly in *One Fat Englishman*, like the infamous barge party on the Delaware River by
New Hope, in which drunken revelers who'd been screwing in
dark corners of the barge kept falling off the boat and having
to be fished out of the water half naked. A lot of the time
Kingsley couldn't remember whom he'd screwed, it meant so
little and he drank so much.

Another pair of Brits doubled the charge the Amises had ig-
nited. Al Alvarez was an explosive nonfiction writer and his
wife, Ursula, distantly connected to D. H. Lawrence, was a ripe
raven-haired beauty who wore her hair long and her bosom
full. Men flocked to Ursula the way women flocked to Kingsley,
but for sex in the opposite mode. Ursula was pure romanticism
à La Belle Dame sans Merci, silent to the point of being sullen.
When she placed a white rose in her bosom, you could hear the
room heave a sigh. Not much later, she ran off with an Irish
poet. The poet's wife committed suicide and Al later attempted
the same, then wrote a book about it. The Alvarezes played out

tragedy while the Amises played out comedy in our small university town of Anglophiliacs.

Adultery was in the air like wood smoke, only no one called
it adultery. It was called Letting Go, and Letting It All Hang
Out, in the jargon of that prefeminist era. Now that Freud and
Kinsey and Joyce Brothers had told us that women were as sexual as men, now that Marx and Marcuse and Norman O.
Brown had told us that sexual morality was the opiate of the
masses, it was a liberated woman's duty not to go out there and
get a job, but to go out there and fuck. We were not at war
with men. Men were our heroes, and we wanted to love them
all, in the high style of Simone de Beauvoir. French women of a
certain class had always had lovers, just as their husbands had.
So had the English. Why shouldn't we?

In food as in sex, America was slipping behind us as Europe
beckoned. The moment classes were over, we all hopped boats
for Europe, often the same boat so that we could continue par-
tying at sea, wallowing in the three large meals a day, wine
included free of charge, plus morning bouillon and afternoon
tea, provided by the Compagnie Générale Transatlantique. In
France, the simplest *casse-croûte*, a sandwich *jambon*, in the
lowliest bar was a revelation of sensuality that put our picnic
sandwiches to shame. We were like amateur painters discovering Picasso. We couldn't wait to get home to marinate fat
shrimp and grill them in the shell so that everyone could peel
his own the way the French did it along the Côte d'Azur.

Food was an index of how far we'd moved into the flesh-
pots of Dionysus, leaving behind the restraints of Apollo. On
our backyard grills we'd long since graduated from hot dogs to
elephantine sirloin steaks, crusty outside and rare within, to be
quilted in garlic butter and served with roasted corn and potatoes wrapped in foil. Now we advanced to butterflied legs of

lamb, marinating them in olive oil scented with herbs from Provence, before we seared them on the grill with thick slices of eggplant. Even the men participated when we spit-roasted a whole lamb for Greek Easter in the American-Greek couple's backyard. Preparing *kokoretsi* of spiced innards or creamy moussaka topped with béchamel and thick yogurt required ethnic know-how, but anyone could take turns basting the naked lamb before we sliced off smoking hot gobbets to wash down with carafes of pine-flavored wine.

When we moved indoors, everything had to be French. We women were discovering with excitement how to upgrade our Irish stews into *boeuf bourguignonne* and *boeuf en daube*. My old fondness for Depression tongue translated into *langue au madère*, brains were *cervelles au beurre noir*, and discarded innards like sweetbreads and tripe were now costly *ris de veau* and *tripes à la mode de Caen*. Now we planned our dinner parties like surveyors exploring new land. When a hostess set forth a *salmis de faisan*, she supplied footnotes on what a *salmis* was. Presenting a *poulet chaud-froid*, she held a seminar to explain how each layer of white sauce was chilled before the next; and how the whole was decorated with medallions of chicken and topped with truffle cutouts before it was shellacked with layers of clear aspic. The ritual of presentation required responsive *aaaahs*.

We were discovering what the French had known forever, that food was like literature and art, and that sex was above all like food. But the subtext was always sex. We wanted to have our cake and eat it too, but we didn't want Betty Crocker cake mix anymore. We wanted *dacquoise* and *génoise* and *baba au rhum* at the end of a Rabelaisian banquet flowing with still wines and sparkling conversation. Every new food opened up new sexual analogues. To explore the interstices of escargots with the aid of fork and clamp, each shell in its place on the hot metal round, each dark tongue hidden deep within the whorls and only with difficulty teased out and eased into the pool of garlic-laden butter—what could be sexier than that? Foods we had known as American but now cooked French revealed a world of innuendo we had missed in our own language. Asparagus that might have gone limp in a steamer stayed stiff with a quick dip in boiling water. Artichokes that had seemed tedious to unleave took on vulvate meaning when the tops of the leaves were cut off and the pith removed and the center made wet with vinaigrette, so that each leaf brought the mouth a step closer to consuming the heart. The canned peach halves that were a staple of my father's table didn't at all resemble the glossy operatic breasts of *pêches Melba*, cushioned on velvet ice cream and rosied by raspberry *coulis*.

On one climactic occasion it all came together—food, literature, sex, and art. Paul and I staged a dinner to honor Muriel Spark, who was giving a lecture series at Rutgers she called "L'Amour de Voyage." She appeared at our little cottage in a chauffeured limo, which impressed us and our neighbors no end. She wore a bright red wig and fake eyelashes that nearly swept her plate and entertained us with bawdy stories while we stoked her with course after course: *oeufs en cocotte avec caviar, consommé à la reine, blanquette de veau, haricots verts, riz à l'impératrice*. By the end of the evening her wig was askew and so were we, but it was all in the cause of Art.

At Princeton, apart from visiting writers, men and women were even more segregated than at Harvard or Yale, where women had infiltrated the graduate schools at least. But if we were ex-

cluded from the classrooms, we were all the more valued for
our sex. In this atmosphere, I capitulated at last. From now on,
I'd be sexy. I made my own clothes, because that way I could
afford expensive fabrics and make a good show. I cut the tops
of my dresses lower and made the waists tighter. I put tissue in
the bottom half of my bras to push my cleavage up. I could feel
men buzz around me like drones to the honey pot, and I liked
that feeling.

I discovered that all I had to do was ask intelligent questions, and men of all ages would find me intelligent. I could
wrap my arm in the arm of the distinguished Eric Kahler, a fellow émigré and friend of Thomas Mann, and while we strolled
across campus feel his pleasure as he discoursed learnedly on
the relation between Klimt and Freud in the Vienna Circle. I
could feel the drama theorist Francis Fergusson glow when I sat
at his feet by the fireplace in his Victorian parlor and asked
questions about Sophocles. I was only half aware that I was
adding new weaponry to my arsenal, the weaponry of flattery
and adoration and argument, not as an intellectual exercise but
as a form of sex.

If I couldn't use logic professionally, I'd use it for fun. With
the lights on, I would engage one or another young male instructor in heated argument over the superiority of Whitman to
Milton, say—the more outrageous the thesis, the better, because it required more skill to defend. It was a fencing match,
the thrust oblique and the parry direct, designed to challenge,
provoke, and parry other thrusts when, lights out, we danced
close and closer to old recordings of "Sunrise Serenade" and
"How High the Moon." So blatantly sexual was argument to
us that the wife of one instructor, a trained nurse, rose from her
chair one night and said, "I know I can't discuss la-de-da po-

etry or the works of Emerson, but I can do *this* . . . and *this* . . . and *this*," and she executed a couple of bumps and a grind that put my mental gyrations to shame.

Dancing, we made love standing up and swaying slow, the way we had in high school and college, teased by the same urges and the same prohibitions, only now it was not virginity we were protecting but marriage. In effect, these were licensed petting parties and there were subtle, unspoken rules about what was and was not permitted. Sitting on laps was okay, dancing so close you could feel each other's body parts was okay. Fondling in public was not, nor was disappearing into bedrooms, but disappearing outside into nature was. Once I sat on our picnic table out back, huddled under a blanket with a vet who'd seen a lot of action in both military and marital wars, a man whose heroism I much admired and whose horniness when drunk was commanding. He got drunk compulsively, as we all did, and when I indicated kissing was fine but that was it, he didn't argue, he simply masturbated while we kissed.

Decades before Bill Clinton's equivocations, we were looking for a presidential solution to the semantics of sex. One evening after a great deal of brandy in front of the fire, Paul and I traded partners with this same vet and his wife. Paul was delighted when we took off clothes, because the vet's wife had unusually large breasts. I hated to be naked because mine had diminished to nonpregnancy flatness, and I was ashamed of them. I was not surprised when the vet proved to be less interested in kissing them than in kissing parts further south, at which point his wife came alive and hit him on the head with her shoe to make him stop. Nudity was permitted, kissing below the belly was not.

Still, when I was cast as the courtesan Bellamira in a student production of Marlowe's *Jew of Malta*, I didn't have a clue how to play her. As a noted Elizabethan drama critic said kindly after seeing the performance, "Oh, I see, you're playing it like Margaret Dumont with the Marx Brothers." Later, I graduated to a full-fledged stripper as the young Gypsy Rose Lee in *Gypsy*. Blinded by a spotlight as I descended a long staircase without a rail in stiletto heels while singing "Let Me Entertain You," I was thoroughly credible as a young girl terrified because she was about to strip down to nothing but a flesh-colored body suit with embroidery in the appropriate spots. That rather summed up the make-believe quality of the sexual games we were playing then. Only years later did Paul confess that during that time he'd been screwing one of his single colleagues at Rutgers for real.

Another visiting writer and his wife became the catalyst for further explosion. Philip Roth's breakup with his first wife, Maggie, left a wild and hungry girl on the loose. She was, as we used to say, dynamite. Roth had not yet written *Portnoy's Complaint*, but he clearly had sex on the brain just as Maggie had it on the body. Maggie, born into the hardscrabble poor of the Midwest, had been a teenage mother and bride in that order. She'd left her children with relatives in order to work and get herself educated, and at the University of Chicago she'd had the good and bad fortune to team up with a manic young writer on the rise.

As a couple, the Roths were far too absorbed in each other to bother with any genteel hanky-panky with the rest of us. They seemed to make war and love simultaneously and with equal violence. But when Roth abruptly left his wife and moved to New York, Maggie was a loose cannon. She was less restrained, repressed, or undamaged than the rest of us, and in her language as in her actions she called a spade a spade. "Come on, I've seen the way you dance with Dave, why don't you fuck him, for chrissake?" she'd ask me. "Who do you think you are, the Great White Ice Queen?" She called me IQ for short. She loved to spar with Paul and me, pitting her energy and despair against our underdeveloped emotions and overeducated brains. The three of us became close, and when Kennedy was assassinated, we took her in to share that long Thanksgiving week glued to our TV, bonded by popcorn and tears.

It was a couple of weeks after Ruby's assassination of Oswald that I saw my first ghost in the cottage. I was asleep in bed with Paul when I woke with a start. In the doorway was a woman in a flowing white nightgown with long sleeves and high neck, her hair loose to her waist, rushing toward me with speed, her face distressed. She came so fast I cried out and hit at her with my foot. It was not until she vanished that I recognized the face of my mother. She came again a few weeks later when we were sharing a log cabin with two other couples and our assorted children at a state park in southern New Jersey. I was sleeping in a lower bunk beneath Tucky when I once again woke with a start. There was someone by my bed. I could feel her, but it was too dark to see. I reached out my hand and whispered, "Mother?" She didn't answer but she didn't seem distressed, and this time she simply disappeared.

Maggie too appeared one night in the doorway of our bedroom, naked. Paul was away and Maggie had come over for supper but was too drunk to drive home, so I opened the sofa bed in the living room for her. It had been an emotional night as the drink took hold, with her trying to call "that fucker" in New York, leaving alternately tearful and threatening messages on his answering machine. I was exhausted when she finally went to bed. But before I could get to sleep upstairs, there she was. "Can I come in?" she whispered. She was crying. Oh Lord, I thought. But I was a mother after all, so I took her in. She immediately took my hand and put it between her legs. "Oh no, Maggie, no, I can't do that," I said. "Please," she begged. I sat up, feeling desperate because I couldn't do what she wanted, but my instinct for survival was as strong as hers. "Go back to bed, Maggie," I said. By that time she'd finished what she came for without any help from me. She thanked me for "being there" and tottered back through the doorway, down the stairs, and into bed.

For a long time, that was my image of Maggie, a long, thick torso on short but sturdy legs, silhouetted against a backlight of trouble. When she tried to kill herself with sleeping pills in New York, I was heart-struck but not surprised. Someone found her in time, but a couple of years later a car she was in plowed into a tree in Central Park. The driver was unhurt, but Maggie was dead.

There were no limits to Maggie's hunger, and there was no assuaging her hurt. I had always said to her, "Whatever you do, pal, don't screw Paul." "I promise," she'd said. And laughed. I felt the current running between them, just as I felt it running between me and Dave McFarlane, a writer who was one of our close friends. But I couldn't explain to Maggie why he and I didn't just do it and get it over with, as she constantly advised. She was talking about sex and I was hankering for love. My hunger for tenderness, for intimacy, for just plain arm-around-the-shoulder affection was too wide and too deep to be appeased by mere sex.

Maggie broke her promise, of course. Sex would win out over friendship every time, as any Guinevere could have told

me. Paul and I had spent a spring vacation week with our children and the McFarlanes in a beach house at Nags Head,
which was no more than a long stretch of sand ending in a
refuge for wild ponies. Paul and I had driven down in two cars,
his Volkswagen and my Renault, because he had to return early
while I stayed on with the kids for a few more days of sun and
sea air and longing to make love to Dave without actually doing so.

I planned to take two days to drive back from North Car-
olina with the kids, stopping at some funny motel with Magic
Fingers mattresses where we could eat popcorn and pizza and
french fries in front of the TV. But we'd started early and made
such good time that it was clear we could be home by dusk and
surprise Paul. When we got home, surprise. No Paul, no car.
But oddly and alarmingly a teakettle was on the stove with a
gas flame under it that had all but burned the bottom out. It
would seem that Paul had left the house hurriedly and hadn't
returned. Had he had some kind of accident? I called a couple
of friends, but they hadn't seen him. I was more puzzled than
worried, so we went to bed, and the children, at any rate, got a
good night's sleep.

At nine the next morning Paul pulled into the driveway and
got his surprise. He'd spent the night in New York, he explained, after Maggie had called to ask us both to dinner. She
was feeling very depressed, so he went alone. And then he
drank too much and didn't want to drive and stayed overnight
because I wasn't due until today. He had no memory of leaving
a teakettle on the fire.

"You mean you stayed overnight at Maggie's?" Maggie was
living then in a tiny apartment in New York.

"Yeah, but nothing happened, it was absolutely innocent. I
slept on the couch."

"You expect me to believe that?"

"What about you and Dave at Nags Head?"

"Absolutely nothing happened."

"You expect me to believe that?"

Around noon I telephoned Maggie and told her I'd come home early and found Paul missing. "Poor baby," she said without thinking, although she assured me that nothing had happened. I could tell from her tone that the reason it hadn't was that Paul had been too drunk. I reminded Maggie of her promise.

It was the thought of that hot teakettle that finally melted the Ice Queen. A couple of weeks later, Dave's wife was called home to Italy when her mother took sick. I called up Dave and asked if I could come over for lunch.

"I don't have anything to eat because Vittoria's not here," he said.

"I'll bring lunch," I said.

He finally understood. "Are you sure you want to do this? You're not just getting revenge on Paul?" I had told him about Maggie.

"I'm sure."

"I have a terrible feeling you're going to hate me afterward."

"I have a terrible feeling I'm going to love you even if I hate you."

And I did, both, for a long time. It was the first of many lunches. We ate picnics outside and inside and all around the town. A decade earlier I had awakened to the sensuality of food and drink, to the aromas, the textures, the explosion of sensation in the nose and mouth and tongue and throat. Now I woke for the first time to the full sensuality of sex. I was as astonished by my body's responses as I'd been by my discovery, on our first trip to France, of the eroticism of Brie so ripe it ran or of ham sliced so thin it was translucent.

"How long do you have?" he'd asked that first time.

"Only an hour," I said.

"Plenty of time," he said, and smiled.

I was insulted. All this extended prelude, all these years of horny desire, and it was going to climax with a five-minute wham, bang, thank you, ma'am? If I was going to sin, in deed and not just in thought, I wanted to sin big. This was adultery I was committing, premeditated and with knowledge afore-thought, adultery in the first degree and not just a quick poke in the dark. I wanted God to know about it.

Dave was taken aback by my passion. So was I—I who was always in public cool and self-controlled. I knew he had had many affairs in Europe, so I was not surprised by his skill, even as I relished it. This was an unknown world. Paul and I had been married for nearly a decade before we'd learned about The Clitoris and then only from a book, which Paul read first and then passed on to me. All that time I'd wondered exactly what a female orgasm was and whether I'd ever had one. Now my body felt like one of my meals, the interstices of ears like snails, the hollow of armpits like the hollow of a pitted avo-cado, the smooth valleys between thigh and groin like a *sauce parisienne*. "How absurd," said my brain. "How divine," said my body. I had flipped myself onto a white-hot grill, and no matter how guilty I felt I couldn't get off. I was knowingly, will-fully sinning, hurling myself on the coals to be seared until juices oozed from every pore, and yet I couldn't stop. Head and body were at total war, and body was bound to win.

I swore I'd never do it again, and in the same breath began to plan the next picnic. We had wonderful picnics. Dave

brought the wine, I brought the goodies. This was my pâté period, inspired by the revolutionary recipes in Craig Claiborne's
New York Times Cookbook. By God, you didn't have to make
Grandmother's ketchup-topped meat loaf, you could make an
authentic French pâté in your own kitchen. I worked through
Claiborne's entire section of pâtés, beginning with one that
doused a five-pound hare and three pounds of pork with a cup
of cognac and moving on to one called Beau Séjour that mixed
pork liver, salt pork, and boneless veal with a cup and a half
of sherry and a cup of heavy cream. My favorite, however,
was the Country Pâté that wrapped ground veal, pork shoulder, ham, pork livers, and garlic in a couple of pounds of fresh
pork fat.

There was still one remaining butcher on Nassau Street,
who, thanks to Claiborne's book, was being inundated by demands for exact quantities of different kinds of ground meats,
some fine, some coarse, and for unprecedented quantities of
pork fat. Fat was an aphrodisiac. Fine Liver Pâté called for
buckets of heavy cream, pureed with bushels of chicken livers
and chicken fat. Truffles, also sexy, were hurled with abandon.
Truffled Pâté, in addition to the usual mix of ground meats and
fat, called for cubed ham and tongue and chicken breasts and
pistachio nuts and a fistful of chopped truffles. We bought tins
of Urbani truffles in the same volume as we bought bottles of
cognac and cartons of cream. It was a time for abandon, and
the rich layered tastes of an unctuous pâté, underlined by a
good Bordeaux, paired wine and food with the rich dark pair-
ings of bodies.

At high noon in the countryside around Princeton, it wasn't
easy to find romantic picnic spots for pairing that were safe
from intrusion by other humans. Like characters in some

steamy soap opera, Dave and I would drive separately to a parking lot somewhere, leave one car behind, and continue together, looking for public land that was private. No simple task—not in heavily populated New Jersey, anyway, where the attractive bits of countryside had long ago been swallowed up in private estates with electric fences and attack dogs. We were reduced to scrutinizing less attractive bits, like the strip of dense undergrowth that lined the Millstone River at the far end of town, near the sewage plant.

Not an ideal spot, but on the other hand there was very little traffic and a car parked on the shoulder would not be noticed. A pair of white bodies entangled on a blanket deep in brush so thick you had to crawl in and out of it would not be visible at all. Picnickers who are determined to picnic will always find a spot somewhere. Ours was full of gnats and mosquitoes, even at high noon, and they were as hungry as we were. I had brought a particularly delicious picnic and had requested a bottle of chilled white wine because we were starting with buttermilk-battered deep-fried chicken—legs and thighs, for the sake of the juicy dark meat—then a salad of avocado and sweet onion and pear in a lime vinaigrette, to be eaten with forks on real plates. And then a quart of Jersey strawberries, topped with a few *fraises de bois* grown in my own garden. I had brought salt and pepper in small waxed-paper packets, and powdered sugar in a much larger packet for dipping strawberries. I brought everything, including corkscrew and cloth gingham napkins, in a wicker basket. Packing each item in the basket had been like putting garments on the body with the intense anticipation of taking each of them off.

It was a hot but not sweltering day, and all went swimmingly until it was time to take off our clothes. We were in

such a thick webbing of vegetation there wasn't room to sit upright, so we had eaten lying down, propped on our elbows, as
Greeks and Romans had done on their couches. And we had
made love as no doubt they had too, only man to woman
rather than man to man. But our blanket was small, and we
kept rolling off into the greenery until rain dampened picnic
spirits and our blanket and our piles of clothes, and we crawled
back to the safety of the car. Next day, a discreet phone call
from Dave to ask whether I'd noticed anything unusual on my
person after yesterday, such as a pink rash. No, nothing, just
lots of mosquito bites. Dave had not been so lucky. His nether
regions back and front had broken out in a poison-ivy rash and
he was hard put to explain to his wife how it had got there.

Breaking out in sin did not cure my Puritan heart, but it
gave shape to my war with myself. Dave, an American raised in
Europe, had trouble understanding what all the fuss was about.
He was puzzled why I was ferocious as a piranha at one moment and the next moment burst into tears. I was strung between desire and remorse, and of course in me the quandary
took literary form. If I was stirring a soup, I would think of St.
Augustine's "cauldron of unholy loves." If kneading bread, I'd
think of Leontes' "paddling palms and pinching fingers." In
my head a scarlet letter blazed. In my heart Christ's words to
the adulteress—"Neither do I condemn thee: go and sin no
more"—were small comfort, because I knew that next week I'd
go and sin some more. What Socrates preached was not true.
Knowledge was not virtue, because I knew what I was doing,
and I knew it was wrong.

I began to understand people who had eating disorders.
They were as obsessed with food and its image as I was with
sex. I understood people who tried to give up smoking and

couldn't. I was one of those myself. I understood people who
tried to give up drugs and couldn't, even though the only drug
we knew, nicotine aside, was booze, and we weren't about to
give that up. I played tug-of-war with Dave and myself, swear-
ing and forswearing, for a biblical seven years. I had always
wondered why everything happened in sevens—seven lean
years, seven fat years, seven years for Jacob to get Leah, then
Rachel, seven golden candlesticks for St. John in his Revelation.
The seven-year itch had turned into my seven-year sin. Maybe
it filled the vacuum left by a disappeared God and Devil.
Maybe I needed an interior drama to enliven the dullness of
housewifery. Maybe it was the one arena in which I could star.

Dave and Vittoria went off to Tuscany every summer, where
Vittoria's family had a villa, and where Dave picked up where
he had left off with one village girl or another. "It has nothing
to do with you and me," he'd say. "I'm like a father to them."
An incestuous father, I muttered, jealous as hell. He was constantly falling in love with their innocence, their swelling bo-
soms, their budding knowledge, and it burned me up that I
knew this about him and still couldn't stop. A couple of weeks
before he left for the summer, I could feel him begin to cool in
order to make the transition easier, like a nomad packing up his
winter tent. Sins must be punished, and if I was betraying my
husband, Dave was betraying me with his summertime girls. He
denied it, of course, but I could tell from his letters, guiltily received and even more guiltily written, mailed in secret, read in
secret, torn into little bits and buried in the trash can, that his
distance was not just a matter of geography.

One summer we rented a house on an island in Greece
through our American-Greek friends, who spent summers with

a small colony of British converts to the Greek Orthodox
Church. It was less Mariolatry that bound them together, however, than the fact that they could live more merrily in a place
that was Not England. The leading convert was a former Oxford don who'd married a Greek villager, another was a remit-
tance man with a title who kept a suitably small yacht and
made love to his boat boys, a third was a widowed engineer
who spent most of his time coaxing an English lawn to cover
sand and rocks, until he persuaded the wife of the don to cover
his bed.

It was a cauldron of unholy loves British style, and we
added our two cents' worth of Americana to the pot. Life on
the Greek isle was one long picnic, under the shade of an arbor
of grapes during the hellishly hot days, under an arbor of stars
during the nights. It was best to be outside, because an abandoned railroad track ran straight through our cement house
from front to back, bisecting the kitchen with its butane-fueled
burners.

In front of the house, a rotting dock extended into the sea,
and once a month we'd be woken at dawn by the thunder of
machinery that hauled containers filled with rocks, on cables
strung from the mountain behind our house to the sea in front.
The rocks were bauxite, first mined during the war, when Mus-
solini's troops had occupied the island and loaded the ore onto
railroad cars on the tracks that now ran through the house. A
black cargo ship hove to beyond the dock to await its load of
bauxite to make the aluminum that once went into weapons
and now went into pots and pans. We were sitting in the middle of a bauxite mine, which lent a special aroma to the heat
that came down each day at noon and turned our "beach cottage" into an oven. I called the place On the Steps of Old
Dachau.

An excess of heat may be the reason I came to grief over mayonnaise in the railroad kitchen. For lunch we walked every day up the hill to a taverna perched in pines above the sea. Here Elena and Georgi fanned their charcoal grills to brisk heat in a tiny kitchen, while their two sons waited on tables set up under the grape arbor, next to pots of small-leafed basil. Here we comforted ourselves with eggs and potatoes fried in olive oil, crunched through ripe tomato and onion and olive salads, savored sweet, crisp octopus caught and tenderized that morning on the rocks, lifted herbed flesh from the bones of grouper or red mullet, slaked our thirst with chunks of red watermelon and spit out the seeds.

On the day of my mayonnaise disaster, the McFarlanes were visiting. They'd driven down from Italy to stay with us for a week, and the visit was not going well. Dave had given few public signs of delight at our reunion, and was avoiding me in private. In the mornings, he'd been writing in a shed out back, where a donkey liked to nibble at the fig trees, while Paul wrote in a bedroom in front. That's what the men I knew did. Men wrote, women cooked, in Greece as well as in New Jersey.

This particular morning, I'd made a cup of Turkish coffee, *metrio*, and took it out to Dave. He thanked me, and that was it.

"That's it?" I asked. "That's all you have to say?"

"I can't talk to you now," he said. "I'm in the middle of something."

"You mean I'm interfering with your work?"

"Exactly."

His work. Paul's old refrain. But what about my work? Come to think of it, what *was* my work? To defer to the men in my life, both of them, to keep the children out of their way so that the writers could flex their minds and imaginations and pump words into sentences to lift paragraphs into heavier and heavier chapters. What *was* my *work*? To please the men in my life, both of them, with the small gifts that women like to give and that the men might or might not notice when they chose to stop work but that the woman knew was a little piece of her heart. Like making fresh mayonnaise for the lobster that we'd specially ordered the day before to eat at the taverna for lunch.

I enjoyed the very thought of whipping together that golden tongue-coating cream tinged with lemon and basil and maybe some wild oregano. But the kitchen was very hot, and so was my anger at being dismissed. *His work*. All this time I had welcomed Dave's love of women as a relief from Paul's fear of them, and yet here I was, back in the box that said, "Don't open 'til Xmas," or whenever play time was instead of real time. In real time, as in war, men worked and women waited. And the truth of that knowledge made me wild.

I took it out, unwittingly, on the mayonnaise. As we know, mayonnaise is based on a physical impossibility made possible by the hand of man. Oil and water do not mix except by circumventing their natures and forcing them together for a time before they revert to their true selves and break apart. The Hellmann's mayonnaise my father placed on the dining table just to the north of his knife, so that he could readily slather it on his iceberg lettuce, his mashed potatoes, his scrambled eggs, his ground beef, his boiled fish, his fruited Jell-O, and his canned pineapple, was kept together for a supermarket length of time by chemical additions. But they were a cheat, and it showed in flavor and texture if you had ever tasted the real stuff.

All you need for the real stuff is a patient hand and a cool

heart, but I had neither when I set out to make mayonnaise for
the lobster. I loved the olive oil we got in the village, so green
and thick it looked like glass when I poured it. I picked some
fat yellow lemons from the tree in the front courtyard. A wire
basket of eggs kept as cool as they could on the windowsill of
the kitchen. That's all I'd need, except for salt and pepper and
the basil I could pick from a pot in the yard and the oregano
from a stroll a few yards further into the rocks.

And of course I would need a bowl and a fork. The fork is
important. Afterward I wondered whether my failure lay in the
quality of the oil or some blemish in the fork. I've made mayonnaise hundreds of times, however, with no more than oil,
egg, and lemon whipped together with a fork. The fault, dear
Brutus, is not in our stars, and I must not fault the fork. Dave
always referred to the gods, Roman and Greek, when speaking
of his destiny. I was too Presbyterian for that. And also too
dang mad.

I started whipping two orange egg yolks with salt and
lemon juice and began to add the green oil, slowly, teardrop by
teardrop, like a woman in pain who is reluctant to show it. I
added the oil so slowly my wrist was getting tired long before
anything came together, because nothing did. Oil, egg, and juice
remained obdurately apart. Egg is supposed to help the oil and
juice join hands by suspending one in the other in a kind of momentary truce. The temperature of all three must be the same,
about as warm as a warm room, in order to create and main-
tain this perilous balance. But what if the warmth of the hand
is such that it transmits that heat down the metal fork and cur-
dles the egg? No matter how long I beat, the emulsion would
not take. I threw it out and started over—fresh yolks, oil,
lemon. No good. I was still working it and me into a froth
when everyone took off up the hill where the lobsters waited. I

said I'd follow them shortly, because, by God, I was not going to let a little egg and oil defeat me.

A fourth, a fifth batch. I grew desperate. Finally I threw in the yolks of the remaining eggs, four of them at once, figuring I could add just a little oil and lemon for flavor and the thickness would be there in the quantity of yolks. This batch looked promising. I clapped on my broad straw hat and dark glasses to make my way up the hill in the blinding sun, and clapped a plate on my bowl to shelter it. When I reached the taverna, my group was already merry from the ouzo and retsina and the smoke of hissing lobsters on the grill and release from the morning's work. My anger dissipated like smoke in a breeze and I removed the plate in triumph to show off *my* morning's work. *Eheu*, as Homer's Greeks were wont to say. The emulsion had broken en route, and clotted green and yellow oil lay like a pool of algae in the bowl.

I didn't need it for a sign, but it was one. When the emulsion worked, it was miraculous but temporary. Neither Dave nor I wanted to add preservatives to make it last. Later that week, we stayed up long after everyone else had gone to sleep, talking softly in the courtyard, drugged by the smell of night jasmine, stretched out on a pair of ancient deck chairs beneath the blameless stars. We could have made love but we didn't. The sky was too big, its fires too remote. We were too small, and our embers too ashen.

On impulse one night just before he and Vittoria were to leave, when clouds covered the moon, we snuck off into a scraggle of olive trees on the hillside and lay beneath them, kissing frantically and without much joy. There was an odd smell when we got up and brushed off our clothes. "Oh my God, goat shit," Dave said. "We've just made love in a pile of goat shit." We who'd played satyrs and fauns in the poison ivy of suburbia had finally pitched Love's mansion, as Yeats said, in the place of excrement.

Yeats's Crazy Jane was as much cook as bawd because she knew that nothing can be sole or whole that has not been rent. As tattered as I felt after Dave's departure, I knew more about love and sex and mayonnaise than I ever dreamed possible from my place at my father's table, to the right of his Hellmann's jar.

Attack by
Whisk and Cuisinart

I STOOD IN THE MIDDLE OF OUR NEW KITCHEN and
fiddled with the lights, dimming some and raising others to
illuminate the croquembouche surrounded by a wreath of
holly on the green baize tablecloth. I shooed Dexter-Margaret
off the tiled counter because she was endangering the gingerbread house with her tail. Votive candles burning in red glasses
lit the framed calligraphic menus on the wall that memorialized
our meals at Lapérouse, Les Baux, Paul Bocuse, Les Troisgros,
Fernand Point, so many medals on the chest of us gastronomic
vets. Mexican tiles on the floor gleamed like old leather. Shiny
copper pots on the rack above the butcher-block island warmed
the oak cabinets and brightened the stainless-steel oven doors
in the wall next to the Garland stove. The stage was set for
Princeton's Annual Christmas House Tour and we were perfect
but for one thing. The croquembouche. The caramel was starting to melt, I could see it sweat. I dimmed the overhead spot.
Forget the star of Bethlehem, candles would do.

The move to the Party House on Lilac Lane had been a

move across town, across caste, across marital divides, across
national schisms. No peace on earth this Christmas. We were in
the middle of a civil war that pitted husbands against wives,
children against parents, friends against friends. War was in
our living rooms every night and in our kitchens every day, as
arguments and tempers rose. Many a dinner party ended with
someone storming out into the night. The Vietnam War had
polarized our small community, as it had others, and I'd become head of the local chapter of a national grassroots organi-
zation that called itself Negotiation Now. Those of us who'd
been turned off by the radical extremes of both hawks and
doves sought to persuade moderates to work for peace. When
my group joined our local congressman in a major antiwar
demonstration in Washington, D.C.—chanting, as we marched
past the FBI building on the Mall, "Fuck who? Fuck Hoo-
ver"—I realized with a shock that this was the first time since
my marriage that I'd been away overnight from both Paul and
the children.

Negotiating with my fellow citizens by phone all day inter-
fered with Entertaining as a Way of Life. Paul hated it and so
did I, but Vietnam had made me fighting mad, mad enough to
organize meetings and protests and petitions and fund-raising
parties. Just when Negotiation Now was preparing to cash in
its hard-won political clout at a Washington conference, however, we were preparing to move households. The friends I'd
been working with couldn't understand why I decided not to go
to the conference. But the move was major for me, too, and
Paul's resentment too blatant to ignore or resist. My job was in
the kitchen, not in the corridors of political power.

We had grand designs for the new house, and we'd hired a
pair of architects to make over the kitchen before we set foot in
it. From the outset, however, it was clear that we and the archi-

tects were designing different stage sets. They saw the kitchen as a showcase of cleanliness for the housewife ruled by Efficiency. We saw it as a combination of French bistro and Provençal *mas*, a backdrop for Grand Entertainments. They wanted the geometry of the Bauhaus, we wanted French Provincial curves. They wanted Formica, we wanted tile. They wanted chrome, we wanted copper. "Why hire us if you don't want an expert?" they asked in exasperation. "If you need dental work, wouldn't you go to a dentist?"

We won out on the mellow oak cabinets with indented moldings, on the glazed Mexican-tile counters and the unglazed terra-cotta floor tiles, which absorbed twelve coats of sealant until I resorted to deck varnish to give them that leathery look. The architects won out, thank God, on the hood, a plain black metal coffin inverted above the six-burner stove next to the commercial gas-fired lava-stoned grill. The hood disappeared as promised, large as it was, into the black background of stove and grill. The industrial exhaust fan of shiny chrome, big as a wheel base, was another matter, but at least it was outside, where its thunder warned the neighborhood what barbecue sauce we were spreading on which cut of pork or beef. We made sure to ask all our neighbors to the kitchen's baptismal party.

We had knocked down the wall between the dark hole of the kitchen and the dark hole of the dining room to create a "living center" for family, for friends, for parties. Flow is what we were after. Now kitchen flowed into dining area and bar and through French doors out onto a slate terrace. Or kitchen flowed into library and parlor and out through another set of French doors onto yet another terrace. By God, we thought, we can party two or three hundred people in this house.

We'd managed to squeeze a hundred or so in for cocktails

and hors d'oeuvres in the cottage, but only if the weather was
good and we could uncork the house onto the minuscule terrace. Our gig there had been to invite an indiscriminate mass
for cocktails and hors d'oeuvres and to ask twenty or thirty
hard-core partygoers to stay on for a giant pot of soup-stew
kept warm on a back burner and a green salad kept cool on the
porch in a dishpan. After word got around, it got harder to get
people to leave and it also got harder to prepare a double menu
of elaborate appetizers and "improvised" buffet because the
hors d'oeuvres were not outside the works, dibs and dabs of
cream cheese and Ritz crackers, but the Works themselves.

Unending platters of hot appetizers were the first line of defense, a display of artillery designed to quell any criticism of
dust under the piano or a dress cut too low. You could make
hors d'oeuvres weeks ahead and freeze them until the time
came to dazzle the assembled multitude with tiny cream puffs
stuffed with creamed crab, mushroom caps stuffed with veal,
Parmesan cheese straws, turnovers filled with Roquefort or
Gruyère, grilled bacon wrapped round a chicken liver or a fig,
canapés topped with cream cheese and salmon caviar, salami
cornucopias filled with sherried Cheddar and skewered with a
toothpick, Roquefort cheese balls rolled in chopped pecans,
tiny tartlets filled with minced chicken livers in a thick
béchamel. No labor was too intensive for such immediate rewards. I relished these secular feasts because they gave me the
illusion of communion, and I cast as wide a net as possible to
bring together communicants on an impulse that was half egalitarian, half ecumenical. As a friend once said, "A Fussell party
is the only place in town where you can shake hands with your
postman, your dentist, and your university president."

With a bigger house I had wanted a children's playroom, big

enough to include the Ping-Pong table, the foosball game, the air hockey board, the carom board, the pogo stick, the Hula-Hoops, the mounting boxes of board games that seldom got played, and the mini billiards table that I longed to buy. The long room stuck onto the back of the house by the previous owner had potential, but Paul commandeered it for his library. With a sinking feeling I agreed, on the promise that we would make a playroom out of the unfinished half of the attic, next to the finished half that was to be Sam's room. We never finished the attic, of course, and it became the cats' playroom as our children grew from tots to teenagers and huddled over their games and TV in a little sewing-and-ironing room on the second floor.

When we gave parties, the kids could pass hors d'oeuvres or sit on the landing and watch the grown-ups, or they could put pillows over their heads to go to sleep when the dancing and drinking went on until dawn. Later on, I trained Tucky and her best pal, Hilary, to be official servers for us and eventually caterers for the dinner parties of our friends. Sam resisted any such recruiting. He kept to his room and made models of Godzilla and Frankenstein's monster or practiced the trumpet until a heavy set of braces ruined his "lip."

In the living center, Paul and I divided the territory between food and drink. Paul's drink space encompassed two sides of the dining area. One side held a built-in wine rack for wines drinkable now, which were the only kind we bought, and the other held a double-tiered cabinet of glass shelves lit from within in order to display glasses and bottles in all their shapes and colors the way real bars did. Around the corner was a built-in ice machine, a prized novelty that was always breaking down.

My kitchen space included a butcher-block island with a deep sink and garbage disposal, pots hanging from a four-sided rack above, a marble counter for pastry making, a second sink and a dishwasher set into a long tiled counter, a professional stove and grill, a stainless-steel refrigerator, and custom-built cabinets designed to hold specialized items like a flour bin and a sugar bin beneath the pastry counter. A shallow vertical cabinet held spices and cans. Deep narrow drawers on rollers held linens, and a set of slots in the butcher block held trays. The counters were high enough for tall people. This kitchen had been thought about, in detail.

The only trouble with this kitchen theater was that we both wanted to star in it. When Craig Claiborne and a photographer came down to do a story on it for *The New York Times*, we vied for their attention. The eighteenth-century scholar grappled with corkscrews, opening wine, while the Shakespearean—that was the hook of Claiborne's story—grappled with a butterflied leg of lamb on the grill. "Sick," remarked one of our academic colleagues on reading the piece in the *Times*, "they're sick."

Sick maybe, showbiz absolutely. Here was a culinary cyclorama designed for happenings as theatrical as Allan Kaprow's, where process was part of the show. Parties were no longer the pretext for sex, and sex no longer the subtext of food. Now food and drink were about power. And cooking—the one activity, besides tennis, in which housewives were encouraged to excel—had become a magnificent obsession.

Dinner parties were important ammunition in the fierce competition among our husbands—and ourselves. While wives in sexy low-cut dresses were still a plus, now the aim was to look like a hot tomato while remaining cucumber-cool within.

You had to keep cool to cook for, lay out, and clean up after parties that required weeks of preparation, parties that consumed infinite time and energy and passion in the one-upmanship of friends.

A key rule of this demanding sport was that she who plays the hostess must also cook and serve. You were allowed some help for serving, but it was a cheat to hire cooking help, especially if you could afford to. If you didn't cook it yourself, the food didn't count. Anybody could hire a caterer. But not everybody could act, and you had first to be an actor in a ritually shared pretense. Pretend there'd been no labor, no expense, no fatigue, no sweat. All dishes, especially showpieces like soufflés, must appear as if by miracle, with a wave of Ariel's wand. And although it was understood among the women guests that each would assist from time to time in shuttling dishes to and fro, no one knew better than we did who'd done the work, and just how much work it was.

But it was work in the guise of leisure. What we were doing in our home kitchens had nothing to do with the calibrated hierarchies, from apprentice to chef, of the professional French kitchen. We weren't about to go off and apprentice ourselves, as a later generation of Americans would, to the great chefs of Europe. Nor were we about to go off and enroll in professional cooking classes, although an occasional foray into Chinese or Indian or some other ethnic venue was permissible. At one point, a group of us used my kitchen for Chinese cooking classes taught by a pro we'd hired to come down once a week from New York. She couldn't understand how we got through so much wine in the space of four short hours, because she didn't realize we were having a party in the guise of a cooking class.

The trick was to be a lady in the dining room, yet an amateur-pro in the kitchen. The distinctions between amateur, amateur-professional, and all-out professional were obscure but vital. An amateur was not skilled. And we were. But a professional was paid for his services. We were not. Like doing other good works inside and outside the house, cooking at any level had to be voluntary to count. To count, that is, in the class warfare that distinguished between blue and white collars for guys and pink and white aprons for gals. Pink signified Volunteer Hospital Aide, white signified cleaning lady. I never wore an apron while I cooked, partly to ease the oscillation between hostess and cook, but also to refuse the badge of household drudge.

The solution to the drudge problem was to make cooking an art, or at the very least a craft, like watercolor painting, embroidery, pottery making, basket weaving, leather tooling, all those genteel accomplishments that distinguished the ladies who chatted in the parlors of Jane Austen from their servants. A lady could become extremely accomplished in any of these arts, even in writing novels, as long as no one took her work seriously or paid money for it, which was much the same thing. Our dinner parties were baroquely elaborated gifts, like the human-hair embroidery of weeping willows and cenotaphs that validated the gentility of Victorian hands.

We didn't want to be professional chefs. We wanted to be artists, and Julia was there to show us how cooking could be elevated to art. We'd called Julia Child by her Christian name the moment *Mastering the Art of French Cooking* appeared in 1961, because she seemed to be talking directly to us. In a very American way, she translated the tools of a traditionally male guild, as regimented and hierarchical as the military, into the milieu of "the servantless American cook," the woman who does her own work. Overnight, she turned our amateur bouts into professional matches within the ropes of our own kitchens. She insisted that if we wanted to do the job right we must have professional tools, the *batterie de cuisine* of a French kitchen. We must equip ourselves the way a soldier must procure his rifle, a carpenter his hammer and saw, a violinist his fiddle and bow, a professor his Ph.D. She sent us scurrying to hotel and restaurant supply houses. She gave us courage to face down even the billy-goat gruff who inhabited the Bridge Company in Manhattan and to demand from him, in our most imperious suburban station-wagon voices, tin-lined copper pots with no less than one-eighth-inch-thick bottoms.

This was no undertaking for the poor. Such equipment cost money, and we weren't looking for bargains. All we wanted, like Jacqueline Kennedy, was the best. Julia warned us away from cheap pots. She taught us that a pot with a copper bottom less than one-eighth inch thick was worse than useless, which meant that a copper wash on stainless steel was there only for show. Out went the Revere Ware at the first Hospital Charity Sale. In came the costly thick copper pots, which were hell to polish if you actually used them to cook in, and which had tin linings that were hell to renew as the tin wore off and the copper came through and potentially poisoned any food that remained too long in the pot.

In came the costly sets of Le Creuset, its heavy cast-iron glazed with red enamel outside and creamy white enamel within, each pot with its special purpose: oval casseroles (*cocottes*) with lids shaped to condense vapor on the roast inside, gratin dishes (*plats à gratin*) that would take broiler heat, saucepans (*casseroles*) with lips for pouring, chef's skillets (*poêles*) with sloping sides for browning, sauté pans (*sautoirs*) with straight sides for frying. Never mind that you had to become instantly bilingual, at least in the kitchen. And never mind that some of the larger casseroles were so heavy they broke your back lifting them from the oven. No sacrifice was too great for the advancement of your husband's career and of your own newfound Art.

A complete *batterie* required specialty firearms like soup kettles (*marmites*), multidisked food mills (*moulins*), vegetable slicers (*mandolines*), double-handled chopping knives (*hachoirs*), wooden-rimmed drum sieves (*tamis*) for creating purees, straight boxwood rolling pins (*rouleaux*), olive pitters (*chasse-noyaux*), fine-meshed conical sieves (*chinois*), poultry shears for deboning chickens for galantines, larding needles (*lardoires*) for barding spaghetti-thin strips of pork fat through a roast, and a complete dud of a metal garlic press sold to the American market before we discovered we could do a better job with the side of a cleaver and the edge of a knife.

We didn't wait for Julia's second volume of instruction to reinforce our initial emplacements. In the affluent sixties, gourmet stores sprouted like mushrooms in the wild. A campaign abroad to purchase arms in Elizabeth David's shop off Sloane Square and in Dehillerin's near Les Halles was obligatory. On our own shores we had already procured a heavy-duty professional mixer, with its wire whip for egg whites, flat beater for pastry doughs, and dough hook for breads and brioches. Only with a mixer could you beat egg yolks with sugar until they formed "a slowly dissolving ribbon." My KitchenAid mixer still stands like a veteran on my kitchen counter, wheezing when called upon to knead a stiff dough, but, like me, proud of long service.

The one sure sign of a Serious Competitive Cook, however, was the copper bowl and wire whisk. You had to have at least one large unlined copper bowl (*bassine*) in which to beat egg whites with a wooden-handled balloon whisk (*fouet*), to foam what looked like snot into a shiny white satin mountain. The chemical reaction between copper and albumin was said to produce creamier and airier whites than could be produced in any other way. So we practiced the specified wrist action, necessary to keep shoulders and arms from aching, with the assiduity of a piano player practicing Bach. We hid our old handheld electric beaters in a drawer, where they pushed our manual Dover beaters to the rear.

The showiest dish you could make with bowl and whisk was a soufflé, the pièce de résistance of our show-off menus and the emblem of our paradox. Literally, the French phrase meant the climax of a series, or a piece of artillery with staying power. A dessert soufflé was a good climax, all right, but its staying power was nil. It held only two or three minutes before collapse. And what was it, after all? An airy nothing, inflated for a momentary display as ephemeral as fireworks, leaving nothing behind but an image in the mind and a memory on the tongue. A soufflé was time's victim, not its resister. And yet, and yet . . . even now I can taste the first *soufflé au Grand Marnier* we ever ate, at a small Michelin two-star restaurant in Paris, Chez Allard, and even now I can remember the pride with which I created the first one in my own kitchen, presenting it in all its quivering brown-crusted puffery before it collapsed within the buttered and sugared eight-cup porcelain mold.

As we moved up the ladder of class and competence, we graduated from plain pâtés to *pâtés en croûte*. It wasn't enough to simply enclose one of our usual brandy-laden mixtures in a crust, or to shape the crust into a hinged oval pâté mold (*moule à pâté*). No, serious climbers had to first bone a duck, leaving the entire skin intact, then stuff it with truffles and pork and veal, stitch it with thread and a trussing needle, wrap it in pastry dough, and decorate it with little pastry fans cut with a cooky cutter to conceal the seam where we pinched the top and bottom pastry ovals together. A meat thermometer, inserted in a paper funnel through the dough and into the meat, told us when the meat was done. And since this was a dish for a cold buffet, we had then to chill the pâté, remove the top crust, take out the duck, take out its stitches, carve it into slices, and tuck it back into the crust. No sweat. See Julia's Volume 1, pages 471 and following.

Veau Prince Orloff was another display piece consumptive of enough money and time to garner status. This one, Julia assured us, could be made in the morning and reheated the same evening—provided you did nothing else all day. It required you to bone and tie a five-pound roast of veal, prepare a *soubise* of rice and onions, a *duxelles* of mushrooms, and a *velouté* from a *roux* enriched with heavy cream and a pinch of nutmeg. You pureed the *soubise* and the *duxelles* together to spread on each slice of the roasted meat, then covered the entire roast with thick sauce and grated Swiss cheese so that it would brown when you reheated it. The dish was so rich that after the first two mouthfuls you were ready to gag or go home, but these were headier times, less obsessed with cardiovascular health and liposuctioned bodies than with strutting your stuff with the best ingredients money could buy.

In food terms, we middle Americans were all nouveaux riches, giddy with a cornucopia of goods and techniques that poured in from Europe, along with its refugees, after the Second World War. To put it another way, we didn't know how poor we'd been until we hit it rich. Rich at the markets in terms of what we could buy, rich in the kitchen in terms of what we were now equipped to prepare. It was a time when more was better and a lot more was best. And so we overdressed our meals wildly and decked them out with too much flash. While the very notion of haute cuisine was new to us, to Europeans it was as old as haute culture, so we went bonkers over all things French. To cook French, eat French, drink French (California wines didn't yet count, and couldn't be mentioned in polite conversation unaccompanied by the word "varietal") was to become versant in the civilized tongues of Europe as opposed to America's barbaric yawp.

The cocktail party with its baroque hors d'oeuvres evolved speedily into the rococo buffet. Julia choreographed the production, plotting the time of preparation for each stage of each dish, detailing what could be prepared ahead, what frozen, what chilled. We each felt we had Julia in our corner, and if your keenest rival led with a buffet of baked ham and roast turkey, you knew how to counter with a *jambon persillé*, presliced and molded into a beautiful green-flecked mountain, or a boned turkey stuffed with veal forcemeat larded with truffles. The more baronial the buffet, the better, and it didn't matter a hoot if guests didn't know or like what they were eating because they could always try something else. My tables were as overblown as a Manuelesque cathedral. No matter how reasonable my initial plan, I always made more dishes, and more, and more, to make sure there was always too much.

Spendthrift of time, I took pride in multistepped preparation that extended over many days and required much special equipment. I delighted in galantines and ballottines because they de-

manded an artist's patience and a surgeon's skill to bone out the
flesh of a chicken or turkey without breaking its skin, to stuff it
and sew it and wrap it and poach it and weigh it and chill it
and glaze it with stock. I jumped at the chance to sculpt a
whole salmon or sea bass into a mammoth pastry crust decorated with scales and fins and mouth and eye, or to paint the
snowy canvas of a *chaud-froid* chicken with a spring bouquet
of vegetables cut paper-thin to resemble flowers. I reveled in
piping the heart-shaped layers of a nutted meringue stacked
with mocha and praline-flavored butter creams and enclosed in
a bittersweet chocolate frosting, decorated with rosettes and
leaves and swags pushed through the various metal tubes of a
pastry bag.

We didn't count the weeks we spent on cassoulets, preparing
what Julia called "the order of battle." Yes, we made our own
sausage cakes of spiced ground pork and Armagnac, and put
up our own duck or goose confit months in advance to have it
ready in its crock of fat, and teased our butcher into getting us
a chunk of fresh bacon and fresh pork rind, and searched for
imported French white beans and then for an earthenware
casserole large enough to hold a pork loin, a shoulder of mut-
ton, the confit, the chunk of bacon and rind, half a dozen
sausage cakes, plus two quarts of beans and vegetables and
wine and stock, covered with bread crumbs and pork fat to
make a crust, which we dutifully pushed under every ten minutes during the baking because the crust, the crust, dear reader,
was the measure of a true cassoulet.

So many parties. So much art down the gullet. Cocktails
with light hors d'oeuvres or with heavy hors d'oeuvres or with
buffets, Sunday brunches and Sunday suppers, tailgate picnics
and beer barbecues and football parties, Christmas Eve and all-
night New Year's Eve and New Year's Day parties. Hangover

parties, birthday parties, political fund-raising and charity parties. Halloween and Thanksgiving and Easter and Boxing Day and Valentine's Day and Fourth of July and Labor Day parties. Costume and theme parties, transatlantic shipboard farewell parties, and welcome-home-from-abroad parties. Formal and informal sit-down dinner parties for four, six, eight, twelve, twenty-four, forty-eight—but that was really pushing it. Each kind of party demanded its own props, choreography, costumes, mise-en-scène, and menus, at a time when women dressed for dinner in long dresses as a matter of course. Often the planning, as in Eliot's *The Cocktail Party*, was more fun than the event, and you worked up such a head of steam getting ready for curtain time that the moment the first guest rang the bell you wanted to go upstairs and take off your clothes and go to bed.

No event was too small to be sanctified by a party. We gave parties back to back: Farewell to the Cottage one month and At Home in the New House the next. The Farewell was to be an informal come-as-you-are party for our regular gang of eight to ten couples, because the rugs were already rolled, half the furniture was gone, and packing cases lined the walls. Perfect for a dancing party. So instead of finishing the packing, I cooked up a *pissaladière niçoise*, with pounds of onions sautéed with garlic and herbs, piled in a pastry shell and topped with anchovy filets and black olives. Then a *gigot de pré-salé farci*, since a boned lamb leg was easy to slice and its rice and kidney stuffing was splendidly exotic. And it was a pleasure to test your skill in cutting into the red flesh to locate the bones—pelvic, rump, knuckle, leg, shank, and tail—because you were learning about your own bones and how the ball joint fit into the hip and how the hipbone was connected to the tailbone and how flesh was covered with fat and fell. *Charlotte aux pommes* was a good finisher, with strips of white bread soaked in butter to line the charlotte mold filled with a thick puree of apples and apricot preserves and dark rum and more butter.

Our Farewell Party was no big deal, but it turned into an all-nighter, what with the dancing and the euphoria, or maybe it was hysteria, of clearing out and starting over. We talked our last guest out the door around 5 a.m., his wife having given up and gone home hours before. So we were a bit groggy when Tucky woke us up at nine to say, "There's a strange man in my bed." Our guest, it turns out, had dropped his keys when he went to start his car and couldn't find them, so he climbed through an open window above the kitchen sink, fell into the piles of dirty dishes, and made his way upstairs and into the first bed he saw. When we went into Tucky's room, there he was, fully dressed and snoring away. That was when I remembered that we had six people coming for lunch.

Our first At Home party on Lilac Lane *was* a big deal, home-cooked food and drink for two hundred. It was a test to see if the flow flowed. While Paul tended bar in the kitchen and guests helped themselves at a secondary bar in the living room, I spread the dining table with a blockbuster array of Julia. At one end of the table, a *suprêmes de volaille en chaud-froid, blanche neige*, the breasts sliced and covered with jellied cream for a checkerboard of black truffles. At the other end, a *mousseline de poisson*, its texture as light as a quenelle, from a puree of scallops and wine and cream and white button mushrooms, shaped into a curved fish and beached on a bed of fresh tarragon. To fill the gaps between: a bowl of *céleri-rave rémoulade*, a plate of endives and artichokes *à la grecque*, a platter of asparagus, the stalks neatly skinned, the heads aligned and scarfed with a *mayonnaise verte*. There was room for a colorful ratatouille and a rice pilaf, baked with butter and minced onion in a Creuset casserole in good chicken stock that I'd made, of course, from scratch.

Always I served two or three crusty French baguettes, sliced for convenience but baked only the day before, at home of course, in the professional black-trough tins Julia recommended, in my simulated baker's oven, in which I created steam by dropping a hot brick into a roasting pan filled with an inch of water. I did not follow her suggestion of buying a piece of asbestos cement cut to the size of my baking rack to create a hot surface, but I did have a couple of leftover Mexican floor tiles, so I used those instead. You got 20 to 30 points for home-baked bread provided it was French or Italian; American loaves didn't count. Croissants and brioche put you up 40 to 50 points, but such tricky doughs were better reserved for small parties. So was homemade pasta, which we cranked out first by hand and then with electric-powered machines, festooning our kitchens with strips of dough of every dimension, on every possible surface, including chair backs and countertops and even the pot rack once the clothes racks were full. The cats had a field day when I made pasta.

Once we had established the mise-en-scène for our kitchen productions, we could focus on costumes. The world was our oyster. For our Moroccan Evening, I served a mountain of lamb and couscous to a circle of sultans and hareems, scented with rosewater and sitting cross-legged on the oriental rug in our library. Paula Wolfert's Moroccan cookbook had given us instant expertise in preserved lemons, which you had to let ripen for thirty days, and in *bisteeya*, for which you roasted and boned a dozen squab, seasoning them with ginger and saffron and turmeric and cinnamon and ground almonds and beaten eggs and cupfuls of butter. It all took time, even if you used phyllo leaves for the pastry and knew you would never ever make a genuine *warka* leaf from scratch. But spending time, your most precious commodity, was the point. Like lust, it was an expense of spirit in a waste of shame.

We had New Year's Champagne parties, Ragin' Cajun Mardi Gras parties, Halloween Apple-Bobbing parties. Sam was not a party animal but Tucky was. She gave a *Jaws* party when the horror movie held our local theater hostage for two years (Peter Benchley was a near neighbor), and she later gave a Speakeasy party with a live jazz band to honor the bad old days before her time when drink was hard to get.

For a long time, I was airborne by party dynamics, propelled by a group rhythm that seemed to obey principles of flight as mysterious as they were inevitable. There was that moment of suspension during the long slow taxi down the runway, the exhilaration when the party gathered speed and took off on its own and you could undo your seat belt and move around the cabin and laugh and drink wine instead of club soda and run up to the attic to the costume trunk to bring back an armful of funny hats so that everyone could be ridiculous and next day call up and say, "Hey, that was some party." Professional chefs, I'd been told, sometimes compared the madness of their dinner-hour kitchens to combat, to the adrenaline-pumped frenzy and release of battle, followed by battle fatigue. Party rhythm was addictive in the same way.

There was even a pleasure in cleaning up afterward. We went through house and yard the next day with an imaginary minesweeper, looking for shards of glass ground into the rug or hidden in the lawn. Ashtrays stinking of stale butts, ashes spilled onto tabletops, half-filled glasses left behind doors and under chairs, a plateful of chicken bones on the piano—even the wreckage had a kind of beauty because it had its place in the scheme of things. The ritual of cleansing was a purgation appropriate to a day of hangover, and it could take most of the day to rinse, load, wash, and empty the dishwasher over and over, until all the glasses, the china, the silverware, the pots and pans were squeaky clean and back in place. Often we fell into bed the second night even more exhausted than on the first.

Those of us who had spent time and money mastering the art of competitive cooking in the sixties found our bowls and whisks suddenly obsolete in the seventies. Just as the Battle of Agincourt turned on the difference between the longbow and the short cannon, so our kitchen wars now turned on the introduction of a new weapon: the Cuisinart.

Carl Sontheimer, an American engineer raised in France, had come across the Robot-Coupe, the Cuisinart's predecessor, at a French cookery show in 1971 and redesigned it to make a foolproof tool for any home cook who loved *brandade de morue* or veal quenelles or scallop mousselines but found them a bitch to prepare. At one blow, it elevated our kitchens to a new level of refinement and eliminated half our lovingly accumulated equipment. Besides chopping, mincing, grinding, grating, slicing, and dicing, it could knead bread, mix brioche and biscuit and pastry dough, puree fruits and vegetables into sauces and sorbets, and whip eggs and oil into mayonnaise.

The Cuisinart didn't alter our ambitions. Indeed, it seduced us into ever more vainglorious attempts to re-create La Grand Cuisine Française in our humble American homes. By this time my bookshelf was packed with the works of nouvelle cuisine evangelists from Bocuse to Guérard. By this time we could buy imported into our own markets the French cheeses and charcuterie and pastries and breads that we'd once gone to France to obtain. Now we could refine our entertainments, as Louis XIV had done when dining privately in his chambers *au petit couvert*, by staging intimate dinners for six. With a few friends, we founded the Princeton Gastronomic Society, which centered on wines accumulated by one of our number during the bargain days of the sixties to be savored drop by costly drop in the boom days of the seventies. We would convene a couple of times each year, after weeks of consultation, to honor *"les vins célèbres"* with a menu to match.

Our dinner menu for March 6, 1976, presented, in order, champagne to accompany a series of *amuse-gueules*; a Montrachet Bouchard 1966, paired with a *mousse de crevettes, sauce Joinville*; a Léoville–Las Cases 1959, for *le gigot farci en croûte*; a *salade d'endives* as a refresher course, *sans vin*; a Richebourg Bouchard 1966 for *les fromages choisis*; a *sorbet au citron* for a second refresher; an Oppenheimer Schloss Müller-Thurgau Kabinett 1976 for *les crêpes soufflés Grand Marnier, façon du château de Meyrargues*; *café*; and, for the insatiable, *eau de framboise*. We were our own chamber opera. We dressed in black tie and dined by candlelight and held our glasses to the light to gaze at liquid that had appreciated to $100 a drop. I removed plates and presented each new platter in my red Thai silk home-designed and -executed gown as if I had spent the afternoon on my chaise, rereading the letters of Madame de Staël. But never was the woman who does her own work more appreciated or applauded for the moment of performance.

That it was only a moment, however, had begun to matter. As with other labor-saving devices, the Cuisinart perversely created more work than it saved. It tempted us into extreme culinary acrobatics, into mousses and purees and *coulis* that once had been too hard to tackle. It pushed us beyond mayonnaise into hollandaise and béarnaise in restaurant quantities, because they were now so easy. It lured us ever deeper into the frozen terrain of *granités* and sorbets and ice creams, with their treacherous meltings and freezings. And it seduced us into *pâte à choux* and *pâte brisée* and *pâte feuilletée*, aerial acts we had never before dared, for fear of falling. But where had all the fun gone? This was hard physical labor, and for what?

The more we embellished our Entertainments as a bulwark against time, the more the Real World as we had known it was in retreat. All the rules were changing. A new generation of boys did not march off to war without protest or evasion, and a new generation of girls said no to the kitchen. The rebellions of the sixties finally permeated even the most fortified walls. While we partied on, Rutgers at last rescinded its nepotism rules, and I finally got a part-time job teaching Shakespeare and Freshman English at Douglass.

The dilemma of Douglass was typical of my own. As an all-women's college, it had gained in stature during the preceding decade until it rivaled all-male Rutgers. Should it now push for coeducation, or should it affirm its own identity? An aggressively active feminist group had formed on campus, and as with other power movements of the sixties, it was either join on their terms or go to the wall. I hated their bullying, feared their anger, resented their arrogance. The ideologues of the feminist movement seemed to me as narrow and dogmatic as the Calvinists of my youth. My generation of women was betwixt and between, too young to fight in one kind of war, too old to fight in another. Men as a group were not our enemies, they had saved our lives, and in gratitude we protected theirs, often at the expense of our own.

True, equal opportunity had got me the job at Douglass
that, inadvertently, saved Sam's life. Just before Christmas, he
was home from school for several days with fever. The doctor
diagnosed flu and cautioned us not to worry. But the fever kept
on and his nightmares became so intense that we moved him
onto a cot in our bedroom so that we could comfort him when
he woke at night screaming. I was teaching *King Lear* in New
Brunswick when Paul noticed that Sam's skin was turning
green. He wrapped him in a blanket and drove him to the hospital, where he underwent surgery for a burst appendix. The
war vet knew gangrene when he saw it.

But many of the gains of the new feminism seemed equivo-
cal to women like me, and despite the commands of young
warriors, few of us moved into full-time careers. Yes, we were
increasingly restless in our kitchens, and many of us tried to
parlay our voluntary services into paid ones. But we didn't
want to be liberated forcibly, any more than the hookers on
Forty-second Street wanted to be liberated by flying wedges of
affluent Women Against Pornography. I was glad for the new
doors opened by affirmative action, but I found it impossible to
shut them firmly behind me. I had invested too much in my
decades of caretaking, which despite its frustrations had meaning to me. I couldn't simply exchange one role for another, so
like countless other women I took on both, doing double the
work in the same amount of time.

We were showing signs of battle fatigue as the conflicts of
the era raged on, not only between generations and genders but
on the home front. Paul and I decided to throw a Come-as-
You-Were-in-World War II costume party as a kind of declara-
tion of truce in the midst of Watergate and Cambodia and a
War gone Bad. But our costumes revealed how far apart we'd

been even in the Good War. Some arrived in bobby sox and swing skirts, others in Boy Scout shorts. One came in a diaper. Those who couldn't squeeze into their old uniforms rented new ones. One slender matron came in the Wave uniform she'd donned at eighteen, an older man in the German uniform he'd worn as a Romanian spy for British Intelligence. Discovery was not in the unmasking but in the cover-up.

Our staged entertainment was the Andrews Sisters, mimed by a pair of actress friends and me, who donned snoods to sing "Boogie-Woogie Bugle Boy," karaoke style, with "Apple Blossom Time" for an encore. Dinner was a canteen buffet: Vienna sausages stuck on toothpicks in a head of cabbage; shit on a shingle (creamed dried beef on toast); Spam grilled, fried, and baked with pineapple slices in brown sugar and cloves; Jell-O with canned fruit stuck in it; a serve-yourself bar with big bottles of cheap rye and gin. We jitterbugged to "Chattanooga Choo-Choo" and danced close to "Sunrise Serenade" and crashed like a 'Nam helicopter as fisticuffs broke out in the kitchen. Uniforms renewed old enmities. An ex-Army sergeant took a swing at an ex-major, who returned the favor, until their wives got them outside and into their suburban station wagons and home.

Paul had worn his old Army lieutenant's uniform. I had made my Uncle Sam costume of red satin tailcoat and navy blue pants to simulate one I'd worn in junior high for a wartime musical pageant. When the last guest left, we looked at each other in our crumpled costumes, a parody of our wartime selves, and sighed. In a matter of seconds, we collapsed in fatigue like individual soufflés. So much work to be done.

The fun not only had gone out of our parties, it had gone out of real life. More and more our Entertainments rang as hollow as the voice of Richard Nixon and as false as the windows with geranium-filled window boxes that city officials had painted on the walls of crumbling slums. For a decade we'd concocted a living theater in the kitchen of our dreams, but now the fabric of our vision was melting into thin, thin air.

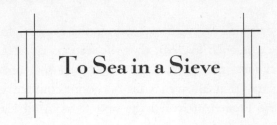

To Sea in a Sieve

IN THE CHURNING BOWELS of the *Liberté*, wedged like a double-decker sandwich in upper and lower bunks in a stateroom so narrow you had to turn sideways to get to the head, we were rocked to sleep by the boom of propellers. While the wake streamed forever behind us, time stood still. For six blissful days we were nowhere, doing nothing. We were at sea.

From the first transatlantic trip Paul and I took in steerage in 1953 to our last in first class in 1976, ours was a shipboard romance. Life at sea was life stripped to the basics—food, booze, sex, books, sea, air, sun. The class-stacked decks, the regimented schedule, the rows of allocated deck chairs, the assigned places at dinner—being at sea had the satisfying order of limited choice, like a prix fixe menu in which you could choose soup or salad, meat or fish, but not the number or order of courses.

Luckily, our most intense period of travel coincided with the golden age of the transatlantic liner after the war. Ships were icons of national glory—the *Liberté*, the *France*, the *United States*, the *Queen Elizabeth*, the *Michelangelo*, the *Leonardo*, the *Staatendam*, the *Rotterdam*—the roster like an elaborate costume party that allowed you to choose country, class, and cuisine. The French provided the best food in all classes, and were the most egalitarian about loopholes and gangways for interclass minglings. So whenever possible we went French.

Like many other culture-starved academics who swarmed the lower decks when travel was cheap, we were looking for a foster country and were torn between England and France. On that first trip, I'd stayed up all night to watch dawn green England's sceptered isle, but my heart was captured at midday by the sunshine of southern France, dappled by plane trees in orderly rows, smelling of wild rosemary and thyme. England was Puritan America intensified by caste warfare, but France, or at least Provence, was California with a sense of history—and a history of the senses. Over the years, we would dip into England for literary duty, then run over to France for food and fun.

Paul found satisfaction in critiquing each product, each meal, each chef, each restaurant, according to the categories of excellence established by the red Michelin Guide, our vade mecum compass and bible. My pleasure was in the hunt, in tracking each comestible to its farmer, fisher, baker, winemaker, goatherd, poultry breeder, truffle hunter, butcher, oysterman, cheesemaker, all those dedicated craftsmen whose work empowered the artists in the kitchen to perform for an audience who understood their art. It thrilled me to uncover layer by layer the world they shared, a bread-and-butter world that at the same time tuned the spheres.

We were united in our quest for the Perfect Chicken, which

we first ate at the three-star restaurant of La Mère Brazier, nes-
tled in a suburb of Lyons. We'd sought her out because I'd read
in Elizabeth David about her *volaille demi-deuil*, a pure white
chicken with slices of black truffle showing under the skin of
the breast to create a "chicken in half-mourning." Brazier had
inherited the dish and the little kitchen knife of Mère Fillioux,
not the actual knife but the skill of carving with it, a knife so
famous in the 1920s that when Mère Fillioux wouldn't sell it to
a pair of metonymy-minded Americans, they stole it from her.
With this four-inch knife, Fillioux had carved half a million
chickens at the tables of her customers during her thirty-year
reign as the mother of *la cuisine de la mère*, and after her Mère
Brazier had done the same.

I still have the notes I took after we'd sampled Mère Brazier's chicken, served simply in a bouillon with pickles, poached
carrots, and coarse salt. I'm amazed how clearly we spelled out
our differences at the beginning of our quest:

> P: Disappointing because not exciting, not dramatic.
> B: Lovely because pure, like a perfect *pot-au-feu*,
> which couldn't be served in anything less than a three-
> star restaurant because it's so simple.
> P: You go to a three-star as you go to a whorehouse,
> for a little excitement. There's little enough drama in life,
> one shouldn't waste the opportunity at a great restaurant
> to exploit brilliance, drama, theatricality.

Mère Brazier granted me—brusquely, but also graciously
considering my wretched French—my first interview. Posing as
a journalist, I asked where she bought her chickens, the famous
poulardes de Bresse. She gave me the name of the farm in the

Saône Valley before lamenting, *"Ce n'est plus pareil"*—"It's just not the same anymore," her elegy for the snowy birds of yesteryear.

But I'd never eaten its like before, so what for her was evidence of Spenglerian decline was for me an epiphany. As I interviewed hundreds of artisans over the next decade in my struggles to become a journalist for real, I learned that her lament was a set lyric piece, a *chanson pastorale*, formulated by Villon centuries before. But all this poetry, all this art, all this passion—over a chicken? How French! How magnificent! How absurd! That's why we were here, to wallow in this emotionally mind-blowing culture that linked gut to brain, art to science, passion and pleasure to ordinary daily life.

If France was about food, England was about drink, and travel was a way to get both without having to spend time in your own kitchen. The Way In, as the sign in Harrods used to say, was the Way Out. England was not only about drink but about getting drunk, in highly codified ways, in order to bridge the moat between Below Stairs and Above Stairs. Everything below the neck, for starters, was Below Stairs, an area of embarrassment and shame, to be kept out of sight like a basement loo. Everything that mattered was Above Stairs, beginning with the head. Above Stairs, wit and malice glittered, especially when stimulated by strong drink.

We'd spent a year in London in the early sixties, renting an eighteenth-century town house from a pseudo Polish countess (real Polish, pseudo countess) at Trevor Square in Knightsbridge, a classy address where our local grocery store was the Food Halls of Harrods. The house was a period classic with one room per floor, connected by narrow stairs: dining room on the first, parlor on the second, master bedroom on the third, second bedroom on the fourth, kitchen and maid's room in the dark, dank, chilblain-inducing basement.

The contrast between Above Stairs and Below was as great as the English could make it. The heating system was equally English, a curious amalgam of coal and gas, which provided hot water for six-foot bathtubs but no heat for radiators. We kept warm by living under the comforters in our layered bedrooms, grown-ups in the middle, little Sam in the basement below us, Tucky in the bedroom above us. When we all came down with what was called in London the Hong Kong Flu, and no doubt in Hong Kong the London Flu, we communicated by rapping on our radiators since all three layers of us were too sick to move. This was the flu that ended at last my struggle with tobacco. I vowed, Dear Lord, if You let me live through this, I promise never to abuse my lungs again. I made no promise about my liver.

The subterranean kitchen was built for dwarves. Its only window was a narrow pane of glass at eye level with the narrow strip of grass in a backyard just big enough for a coal bin. The kitchen was underequipped for anything but boiling water for tea. It had an electric teakettle, a brown china pot, a quilted tea cozy, and two kinds of sieve, a fine-meshed strainer with a silver rim for formal service at the parlor tea table and a hinged pair of perforated metal spoons to contain loose tea leaves when you made a single cup for yourself. Tea bags had not yet displaced the rituals of a proper cup of tea.

A staircase not quite as wide as my hips connected the kitchen to the dining room above. So did a dumbwaiter. A buzzer concealed beneath the rug at the head of the dining-room table summoned the kitchen dwarves to haul and serve. The dining room sported a showy chinoiserie highboy lac-

quered in the same shade of red as the walls, on which a skilled
Italian sometime in the nineteenth century had painted murals
of Venice à la Canaletto. He had also painted Venetian scenes
on the table itself, along with the dining chairs, in turquoise
and red and gold. In such a setting food was superfluous, even
counterproductive, as I discovered when I actually tried to use
the table as a table. Our landlady instructed me: Cover the
table first with boards encased in quilted padding, then with a
thick undercloth, and finally with a tablecloth. The pains we
took scarcely mattered in the end. Our landlady had a fifty-
page inventory of the goods and chattels in her showpiece and,
on completion of our tenure, found some way to charge us for
every one of them.

If our countess thought we were American scum loaded
with money that was her birthright, not ours, a few English literary folk decided we were socially acceptable and that was
enough. We were acceptable because, as Americans, we were
hors de combat. We could be oil riggers from Texas or share-
croppers from Arkansas, as long as we were not coal miners
from Manchester or shopkeepers from Brighton. Like licensed
clowns, we didn't count any more than food counted in the
Great Game of Snobs. The English rules for this game were as
baffling in their minutiae as pub hours and the distinctions between saloons and public bars, but we were off the board and
therefore warmly received.

Over the years, we'd become closer to Kingsley Amis and
his second wife, the writer Elizabeth Jane Howard. We became
semi-permanent houseguests at Lemmons, the expansive
Georgian house outside London that Jane had restored single-
handedly, with much patience and thousands of pounds, to
something of its former splendor. In marrying her, Kingsley had
married Up. Where Jane ruled, the rules were absolute. She

didn't speak to Paul for two days because he didn't listen when she warned him not to pass the bottle of port to his left and not to lift it from the table. She persuaded Kingsley to have his shirts made at Turnbull and Asser and his suits tailored on Savile Row. She completed his transformation from Angry Young Man to Colonel Blimp and later to Thatcherite Conservative. But she could not, no matter how she needled, wheedled, or slaved to feed guests at the great round table in their country house kitchen, alter his mind about food.

At Lemmons, Jane cooked and Kingsley drank. Houseguests like us served as spectators and buffers in kitchen wars that made our own seem placid. No matter whether Jane served a *blanquette de veau* from Escoffier or a steak and kidney pie from Mrs. Beeton—equally delicious, because Jane was that rare thing in an Englishwoman of her class, an excellent cook—Kingsley's bottle of HP Sauce was always by his side and used at full tilt. Each had met his match in the other, and their battle of wills, played out in restaurants, tavernas, pubs, salons, kitchens, bedrooms, and baths, sustained them for years.

When it came time to repay their generosity with a dinner party at Trevor Square, I was up a creek. We'd hired a daily to do the housekeeping, Phoebe from South Africa, who was small enough to inhabit the kitchen but was not a cook. How to cook and serve a dinner party in that house without dwarves or Phoebe was a problem without a solution, but with typical American bravado I blundered ahead. My first mistake was to attempt a classic English menu. From Harrods I bought canned turtle soup of high quality, to be spiked with sherry. From Cobb, the best butcher in Knightsbridge, I bought a saddle of lamb with the kidneys attached. For the rest, I would make scalloped potatoes and fresh peas, with an English trifle for dessert. The beginning and end were simple enough. It was the middle that would require cooking in the underground cavern in an oven that, I discovered too late, never got above 200 degrees Fahrenheit. Result? The potatoes were glue, the peas bullets, and the lamb was half raw and half scorched from my attempt to fry it on top of the stove.

Serving was even more challenging. We were eight at table, dressed in formal suits and long gowns. Ignoring the useless buzzer at my feet, I would run downstairs, throw food in the dumbwaiter, work the pulley, dash back upstairs, tripping over my skirt, and serve. When it came to the saddle, all I had to carve with was one stubby knife with a dull blade. I was whacking away at the backbone when the entire roast slid off the platter and onto my neighbor's lap. With impeccable English courtesy, he asked if he might help me carve. Fortunately by this time even the cooked parts of the lamb were cold, so at least my grease-stained guest was not burned. The party ended with port and brandy in the parlor upstairs, where the hostess drank far more than was good for her and suffered heartburn once the guests were gone. If this had happened in France, like Vatel I would have thrown myself on the stubby blade of my sword.

For over a decade we shuttled between England and France, but as the children grew we went to France more often, for beach time at Collioure or Bandol, and finally, in 1965, to live for a year in Cimiez, a residential district above Nice where Queen Victoria had come to visit and Matisse to live. The Greeks had established a beachhead at Nice, naming it Nikea, two hundred years before Christ. The Romans had left the ruins of an arena behind. Nice was now a big city, part Old Town, part New Town, part Italian, part Provençal, part En-

glish, clustered around eighteenth-century arcades in deep burgundy and baroque Edwardian hotels in white, fronting the
long promenade along the Baie des Anges built by English as
the Promenade des Anglais. It was the right place for Anglo-
Francophiliacs.

The Old Town I called Black Nice, for its winding dark
streets thronged with dark Mediterranean people, shops with
bloodied carcasses in the windows, bars full of smoke and cognac, the Chapel of the Black Penitents opening suddenly on
the brilliant colors of the Flower Market. I took notes on where
to get what. The best vegetables were sold by a man and wife at
their stand opposite the clock tower of the Lycée. The best fish
was sold by the man with the high forehead and big teeth. The
best charcuterie was the one that sold stuffed pork every Saturday at the far corner of the Flower Market. If you knew where
to ask, you could have *brandade de morue* delivered to your
kitchen door every Friday. Salt cod pureed with heavy cream
and olive oil was once a Catholic Lenten dish, but I overcame
native prejudice.

On the borders of Old Town was the weekly market, set up
along the quais of the river Paillon, always a mob scene among
the pyramids of lemons and eggplants and melons, braids of
garlic and baskets of fish, with business conducted so freneti-
cally in Provençal slang that my kitchen French was useless. I
had to point to an enormous wheel of the local cornmeal pan-
cake sold by the buxom Niçoise on a street corner and hold out
coins to buy a slice.

New Town, or White Nice, glittered with light and air, with
solid bourgeois couples walking their dogs along the promenade, ignoring the matronly transvestite in pearls and basic
black who sat on the same bench every afternoon in the Jardin
du Roi Albert Premier. Both towns came together in the Place

Masséna at Carnival time in February, when for a full two
weeks the place went berserk. Cavalcades of ladies and gents in
eighteenth-century costume riding white horses were followed
by men walking inside giant puppets, *les grosses têtes* of papier-
mâché shaped like giant chickens or leeks twenty or thirty feet
tall. Floats enacted grotesque scenes of fantasy or political
satire involving the caricatured heads of Kennedy, Khrushchev,
and De Gaulle. A Rabelaisian Lord of Misrule presided over
all, amidst waves of confetti the crowds threw with such vigor
that you had to wear dark glasses to protect against blinding.
We deployed gentler weaponry in the Battle of the Flowers,
hurling carnations and marguerites at the pretty girls on pretty
floats of flowers, so finely wrought they made the Pasadena
Rose Parade look tacky. Nice knew how to throw a party, and
we felt right at home.

We were living in a house with the lovely name of Villa les
Marguerites in the midst of a walled garden on the Chemin des
Pins. Our landlady and her husband lived in an ordinary house
directly below us on the steep hillside, and despite their uncon-
ditional contempt for Americans, they rented to us on condition that we pay the year's rent in advance—in cash. We called
them Les Fascistes because they attributed all their ills to the
death of Maréchal Pétain. Monsieur was openly hostile and
paranoid, and when we were away, he sneaked into the villa to
check up on us, which we discovered when he accidentally
broke off his key in the front lock. Later he charged us for the
pane of glass he'd broken in order to open the door.

It was Madame who hired for us our first cook, Madame La
Fou, as we called her in our ignorance, not knowing it should
be La Folle. It was unthinkable to Madame the Landlady that
anyone could live in a villa with such splendid public rooms—

walls of turquoise brocaded silk, gilded furniture of Louis
Seize, rugs of oriental weave, toilet seats of Delft porcelain—
and not have a servant to cook and clean. She was protecting
her investment, and besides, it would take a native servant to
know how to cook in a narrow corridor of a kitchen with no
equipment, in a house heated by an ancient coal furnace in a
basement that could only be entered through an outside door
on the street. Madame La Fou presented herself as a cook from
the North, exact location unspecified, who had presided for
twenty years over the grand table of a monsignor. Madame the
Landlady accepted her on the spot. All we had to do was pay
for her.

Because she was from the North, she had no place to live,
and she demanded that we set up a cot for her in the basement.
In America we'd had plenty of cleaning ladies but never a live-
in anybody. Paul hated the idea of a stranger hanging about,
but there was no help for it. Next she demanded that we buy
her a *batterie de cuisine*. Impossible to cook without the items
she'd listed, on several sheets, in a meticulous hand. I went to
Madame the Landlady with concern because the list was so
long and I didn't have Julia with me to tell me what things
were. I could look up *chinois* and *tamis de crin* in a dictionary
and find out that they were sieves, and I could translate their
names literally, "Chinese cap" and "horsehair drum sieve," but
what did that *mean*? It seemed there were sieves and sieves. The
sieve shaped like an inverted Chinese coolie hat had a cone of
very fine mesh or perforated metal or even felt, attached to a
metal rim, and was used for straining the seeds from a fruit
puree or egg whites from clarified consommé. The drum held a
mesh of tightly woven horsehair between a pair of circular
wooden frames, through which you pushed ingredients with a

mushroom-shaped wooden pestle, aptly called a *champignon*, to create a smooth paste, puree, or sauce. Were these esoteric instruments really necessary?

To my surprise, Madame the Landlady said *oui,* and agreed to pay. It wasn't that she suffered a sudden fit of generosity, but rather that she had a Frenchwoman's overriding sense of the *dignité propre à la cuisine*. The kitchen itself had no dignity at all. It was a squalid greenroom for the furious Comédie-Française performed at the dining table by Madame La Fou each noon. And what a performance.

For two to three hours, while all of Nice and Cimiez and the adjoining villages up and down the Corniche retired to their houses to eat the big meal and sleep, we sweated to keep up with the onslaught of dishes served course after course by Madame La Fou. Now that she was properly equipped, she could make a silken pâté out of any sow's ear, tail, or hoof. She worked herself into a lather with her *tamis* and *chinois*, her *braisière* and *bain-marie*, her *moule à douille* and her *pots de crème*. Her cheeks fiery, hair tight in a bun, she mumbled and sighed as she presented each dish, then hovered over us as we took the first bite of an angelic *coquilles Saint-Jacques au vin blanc* or a seraphic *potage à l'oseille*, waiting for the praise we lavished upon her in vain. She knew her food was incomparable and we were unworthy of it. We were not French. Not French from the North. Her contempt for the French of Provence was as intense as Madame the Landlady's for the Americans of Nouvelle-Jersey.

Our children were also required to eat a two-hour meal, but at school. If they did not clean their plates, they were rapped by knuckles on the back of their heads and kept at table until they finished. This may be why my daughter will eat almost anything set before her and my son almost nothing, unless he has

chosen it himself. After the noon dinner, they played unsuper-
vised in the schoolyard, where the Americans (only my two)
and the *pieds-noirs* (of which there were many) were pitted
against the French in an ongoing battle fought with palm
staves, while the teachers enjoyed their meal at leisure.

The dark side of the French obsession with food became ev-
ident when Madame La Fou began to grumble about her basement quarters. She'd insisted that all she wanted was a cot, but
now she wanted to move upstairs into the guest room. She also
began to exhibit signs of our landlord's paranoia. "They" were
after her, she explained, with sweat beading her upper lip. We
knew she had left behind a husband and children, as well as the
monsignor, but she declined to say why, except to imply that
something terrible had happened. Poison, I speculated, having
just read Mauriac's *Thérèse Desqueyroux*, set in the North. I
didn't want to get on her bad side, but I knew I wouldn't sleep
a wink with her in the room next to us. I'd become truly afraid
of her. After a particularly sullen lunch, I consulted Madame
the Landlady. "*Parbleu*, I fired her this morning," she said in a
rush. "She came to me with the most extraordinary demands!
The woman's demented—I wouldn't be at all surprised if she
was wanted by the police—so I gave her twenty-four hours to
pack and get out."

I told the children to lock their bedroom door in case
Madame La Fou attempted to sleep upstairs on this, her last
night, and entered their room by mistake. We locked our bedroom door and that of the guest room, which we could enter
via an adjoining balcony. She could climb up to either balcony
by means of the wisteria vines that arbored the terrace, but she
had considerable poundage to haul, so we felt relatively safe.
We heard nothing during the night and the next morning she
was gone, without a sound, without a trace, leaving behind a

dignified *batterie de cuisine* and a faint sulphurous whiff of madness.

The next cook we hired ourselves, making sure she didn't want to live in. Madou had been working since she was twelve in the hotels and restaurants of her native Médoc. She was in her forties and came no higher than my waist, but she could do anything. She could stoke a furnace, fix a faucet, light the oven without explosion, sing lullabies to the children, and puree through the *tamis* a *soupe de poisson* equal to any in Marseilles. And she liked Americans. They were nicer to her than the French were.

She insisted that I check all grocery accounts item by item and, once she understood that I trusted her entirely, allowed me to accompany her on her shopping rounds. In her little green coat she buzzed like a fly through the produce of one corner market after another, through the local *poissonnerie, boucherie, boulangerie, charcuterie, pâtisserie*, alighting here and there to greet, poke, sniff, sample, palpate, negotiate, laugh, and commiserate before moving on. Each purchase was a litany intoned at breakneck speed because it was as fixed as curtain time, five days a week. "*Bonjour, mesdames,*" sang the mussel seller and her husband, holding up a string bag of silvery black shells freshly washed in a mussel-cleaning machine. "*Bonjour, madame, bonjour, monsieur,*" sang Madou in response. "*Comment ça va? Tout va bien? Ils sont tous frais? A quel prix ce matin? Ah, quel horreur.*" The quick flutter of fingers over the shells, the quick counting of coins and bills, the ceremonial departure. "*Au revoir, mesdames, merci bien.*" "*Au revoir, madame, au revoir, monsieur, à bientôt.*" And then on to the carrot lady, the lettuce man, the cheese and milk couple, the butcher, the baker, the candlestick maker. I was mesmerized by the ritual.

Once back at the villa we deposited our string bags, lumpy with purchases, in the kitchen. Then I was banished to the parlor because I got in the way as Madou whirled around the narrow space like the blade of a Cuisinart, turning all this provender into the day's salads, sauces, soups, roasts, filets, omelettes, side dishes, and desserts, in a dreamscape where the baguette was always crisp and the butter ever sweet. Unless it rained, and it seldom did, we ate on the terrace underneath the wisteria, so my memory is tinged violet and perfumed by the roses and hollyhocks and little yellow marguerites of the garden. After lunch, we staggered upstairs for siesta, that most luxurious and un-American of rituals. We closed the tall wooden shutters over the French windows, but there was still soft light and plenty of time to read and lazily make love and even sleep.

Nothing in Nice or Cimiez reopened until four in the afternoon, when we woke to the drone of motorbikes and motor scooters swarming through the narrow streets. Madou had gone, leaving the kitchen and the rest of the house immaculate. She had set the dining table for tea, which I served after I fetched the kids home from school at five o'clock. She had put out bread and soup in the kitchen for supper at eight. The soup was invariably a puree of leftover vegetables and meat juices, put through the *tamis* and enriched with a large pat of butter. The soup was as soothing as our daily routine, which, because it was almost as regimented as life aboard ship, seemed to stretch time instead of frazzle it. It was a good way to live.

With a real cook in the kitchen, I had time to pursue a different kind of kitchen work. Every morning after shopping I walked down to the Nice Public Library and dived into the ocean of French gastronomic literature. In France food not only had a history but a literature: Ali-Bab, Curnonsky, Dumas, Grimod de la Reynière, and of course Escoffier. Escoffier had been born in a village just down the road from Nice, at Villeneuve-Loubet, and his house there was being restored as a museum.

I interviewed the curator, eighty-year-old André Layet, a native of Villeneuve who had worked under Escoffier at the Hotel Métropole in Monte Carlo before following him to London. All the paintings in the museum had been done by chefs, including one by Layet called *Dream of the Old Chef*. Many chefs were painters, he said. Chefs were good with their hands.

To interview any chef, retired or otherwise, was to experience a living tradition of art that was entirely about food. Everyone I talked to seemed to share this tradition, and it blew my mind. Monsieur Verdoja, proprietor of our favorite local bistro, L'Estragon, where we dined as a family every Sunday night on *sole meunière* on the bone, "good value for under 12 Francs." M. Augereau of L'Auberge Jeanne de Laval at Les Rosiers-sur-Loire, whose meals were so perfect that we stayed a week in order to eat them twice a day. M. Claude at L'Auberge d'Hostellerie des Santons in Grimaud, who had just won his first star. The venerable M. Tuillerie at L'Oustau de Baumanière in Les Baux, who had won his three stars decades ago. The modern revolution of celebrity chefs was in its infancy, and chefs were happy to sit down and share a glass of champagne and a half hour of chat with an eager American questioner.

By now, Paul and I had eaten the Perfect Chicken not only at the inn of La Mère Brazier, but at the restaurant of La Mère Blanc in Vonnas-sur-Veyle. One weekend, with the children safe in their beds at Cimiez, we set off in the yellow Beetle to track it to its source in the area of Bresse, birthplace of Brillat-Savarin, northeast of Lyons. It was beautiful countryside, with tile-roofed farms scattered across the sunbaked earth like grains of maize, and everywhere the hum of bees. We had to ask directions many times of blue-smocked farmers on horse-drawn carts, but at last we found the farm of Monsieur Cyrille Poncet, president of the Club des Lauréats of Saint-Etienne-du-Bois. It was a rustic slab of a house with great bunches of maize hanging from the eaves. The door was open and in the dark inside sat an old man and an old woman, each in a black felt hat, eating silently from a bowl.

Poncet spoke in a country dialect, but I taped him so that I could translate his words slowly at home. His grandfather had competed in the first *concours* of the birds at Bourg-en-Bresse in 1862, honoring Napoleon III. His father had won the *prix d'honneur* six times, for a breed that had been known since the sixteenth century and had been granted a government appellation since 1936. "*Beauté et qualité*" was the motto of the prize-winning Lauréats. "To keep the purity of the breed" was the passion of the Poncets. He described how his wife caponized the birds the way the Romans had and lovingly force-fed them a paste of corn and milk in their Death Row days. He showed us how he prepared them for exhibit by pushing in legs and wings to make a smooth white blimp of the body and to show off the blue legs, wattles, and combs. "Demand the Standard," Bresse producers urged, "the Bird with the Steel-Blue Legs."

These were not the chickens of my forefathers, these birds with breasts thick, tender, and juicy—"succulent as a woman's," as Paul Bocuse had said—but I was struck nonetheless by the rod of conversion. At last I had something to write about that was not just literature but life, that was not just for today but that bore a history as old as ancient Rome, that was not just intellectual or sensual or artistic but was all of these rolled up together, something that was remarkably like love. Who but the French would make a chicken a love object, would caress it with the passion of a lover for his beloved or a communicant

for his God, would turn it into a work of art that, no matter
how crowned with laurel, must be eaten to be experienced?
"Like the wines of Burgundy, it is on the palate that one appre-
ciates them," said M. Poncet of his birds. "The rest is words
in the air." What a revelation! I took up my primitive tape
recorder and my portable typewriter and began to put words
on paper.

Every chef attributed his art to the quality of what he
brought into his kitchen from local purveyors. So I sought out
André Pio on his small vegetable farm at the mouth of the
Loup, les Frères Guigues at their butcher shop in Old Town,
Pierre Armand at his fish shop in Place François, and Hans
Brobecker at his bakery on rue Marceau. They all sang the song
I'd heard from Poncet when he extolled the beauty of his chickens and the honor of his *métier*. Each had a calling that gave
meaning to his life. I heard echoes of Isaiah's "Here am I; send
me." It was a love song, a *chanson d'amour*, that fed their
souls.

By the time we'd undergone initiation into the *ancien régime*
of Lasserre in Paris (to eat *truffe sur la cendre*) and La Pyra-
mide in Vienne (to eat *fois gras en brioche*), we felt ready for
the Young Turks of Nouvelle Cuisine. Paul and I took a weekend trip to Lyons to sample the work of a promising young chef
I wanted to interview because he'd just won his third Michelin
star, Paul Bocuse. With his own Perfect Chicken and his
saumon en croûte, Bocuse did not disappoint, nor did he intim-
idate. He not only liked Americans, he liked America. He invited me to spend a week cooking in his kitchen, but I had to
get back to the kids, so he invited us into his playroom downstairs, where he'd constructed a Western movie saloon with
player pianos and shotguns and ten-gallon hats. While we were
playing at being French, he was playing Cowboys and Indians.

When we got back to Nice, Madou was in a tizzy. A thief had hit seven villas in a row the night before, making headlines for the *Nice-Matin* as *"le Voleur des Villas."* He was a skilled second-story man who had left his ladder in our garden as evidence that he had tiptoed past the children's bedroom upstairs, where Madou was also sleeping, to ransack Paul's study downstairs in the vain hope of jewels and cash. He had better luck in our landlords' house, where he'd made off with a sackful of jewelry but couldn't get at their cash, locked in the cupboard of the room where they were eating. He'd buried his loot in the garden of the seventh villa just before they caught him and put him in the very jail where Madou's boyfriend was a cop. All the cops and crooks of Nice knew each other because they were all from Corsica. Unfortunately, the salary we paid Madou went straight into the pockets of her cop, a compulsive gambler who spent all his time outside the jail inside the casino.

Madou it was who saved me during my *crise de foie*. *"Ma foi, mon foie,"* we used to joke, because Madou ascribed every ailment from a sick headache to an aching back to the liver. But it was true that *ma foi*, in the medieval Christian sense of fidelity, was in poor shape. I was still corresponding, fitfully and guiltily, with Dave. I received his letters at the Hotel Vendôme on rue Pastorelli, heart pounding, certain the desk clerk knew I was having an affair—he was French after all—and certain that each letter, like each cigarette in my smoking days, would be my last before I quit for good. So when I was knocked out by lobster poisoning, a bad liver seemed an appropriate punishment for bad faith.

Once again the trigger was a lobster—not a true *homard*, but the common European crayfish, langouste. A *langouste niçoise*, in fact, which according to a famous Niçois gastronome was the true origin of the dish mislabeled *homard à l'américaine.* The langouste in question was the orgasmic climax of a long-awaited meal in our favorite of all restaurants, Chez Puget. Here the ritual was liturgic: the burgundy drapes on the windows, the mauve walls, the pink linen on the tables, the black silk bosom of Madame Puget on the cashier's counter, the white toque of Monsieur Puget in the kitchen. Chez Puget was consecrated to the proposition that all virtue, art, and glory are expressed in France's classic bourgeois cuisine.

Here we learned the *alphabet sacré* of *aïoli, brandade,* and *cassoulet.* We learned that vegetables were always served on separate little dishes. We learned that the secret of what we called "the caramel sauce" was foie gras stirred into a *glace de viande.* I'd interviewed M. Puget near the end of our stay and he'd promised to create a menu especially for us. Because of subsequent events, I've blocked everything but the glorious langouste, served in the two halves of its shell, the flesh wet with oil and garlic, cognac and tomato, a Mediterranean melody in every bite. We fell all over ourselves, in a dignified French way of course, expressing gratitude to Monsieur and Madame and to their children and to the descending row of kitchen help, before bidding adieu. By the time we reached our car, my belly was tied in a Gordian knot.

"Drive fast," I urged Paul, "or I'm not going to make it." When we reached the villa and I stepped from the car, I exploded in both directions. Paul had to carry me into the house and into the downstairs john, where the Delft porcelain toilet and sink were adventitiously cheek by jowl. I stayed there until all my insides were out, then crawled up the stairs and passed out on the bathroom floor. I woke up in bed, where I stayed for a week, with Madou hovering over me with now a cup of bouillon, now a cup of tea, and whenever I opened my mouth another teaspoon of Fernet Branca. She was doctor and nurse, and although I had no idea what a *crise de foie* was, I recognized a severe but not fatal case of shellfish poisoning. That meant the worst was over.

I stayed clear of crayfish the rest of our time in France, but when we came back to the States the thought of never again tasting lobster was unbearable. I speculated that my reaction was not to the shellfish itself but to what it might have fed on off the coast of North Africa, which exported large numbers of crayfish to France. The next time Paul ordered a Maine lobster, I took a chance, took a bite, and suffered nary a twinge. I sent a thank-you up to God. I would not have to sacrifice lobster as punishment for my sins. A week of purgation had been penance enough.

In the mid-seventies, we decided to have one last fling on a transatlantic liner, and this time to do it in style, first class on the SS *France*. But the first night's dinner, for which we'd dressed with exquisite care and paraded down the staircase of the dining room with movie-star panache, was a disaster. A miserable fruit cocktail, a dried out turbot, a shriveled slice of turkey ballottine, a fatigued cheese served with saltines. Saltines! Paul took it as a personal affront. I remonstrated with the maître d'hôtel that the meal was execrable. "*Comment?*" he inquired, puzzled. I repeated the word. "Ah, *exe-crable*," he repeated, with the accent on the penultimate syllable, laughing and nodding in agreement. "*Mais oui, mais oui, madame, exe-crable.*"

The joke was on us. Even though it was possible to order special dishes off the menu, the *quenelles de brochet* were rubbery, the *saumon au beurre blanc* mushy, the *gigot d'agneau* stringy as old tennis shoes. Only the drink was reliable, for

which you paid extra, of course, and heavily. Our table companions were no comfort when they bragged that the meals
they'd had on TWA were far superior to anything they'd had at
Lasserre. After dinner the bars were empty, and in the once
spiffy Café d'Atlantique the hired pianist played "To Dream the
Impossible Dream" to a sole listener, a school librarian in
brown chiffon.

Our swan song to the sea voyage was a Swan cruise from
Southampton to Nice, to which we'd been invited by Kingsley
and Jane, who'd been invited in turn by the writer Anthony
Powell and his wife, Lady Violet. I figured afterward that the
Powells had wanted the Amises along as security against in-
truders, and the Amises had wanted us there to distract them
from their disintegrating marriage. We were a set of nesting
lifesavers, but none of us were safe on our Journey to Disaster
aboard the MTS *Orpheus*, with port stops along the western
coast of Europe—Brittany, Spain, Portugal—until the ship
reached its home port in Nice, from where it could take off on
its regular Hellenic route along the eastern Mediterranean.

We descended to D deck, D for Dionysus, D for Dungeon,
back where we'd begun on the *Liberté*, just above the vibrating
propeller screws, but at least the noise dampened the shouting
of the Amises in the cabin next to ours. The "welcome dinner"
was a tip-off: canned fruit cocktail, library paste soup, drip-
dried fish, greasy duck, unripe tomatoes, melted ice cream. The
Powells, I noted, took fruit cup and soup and went straight to
ice cream. Wine was extra, of course, and the Powells' rule was
that each couple was to order and pay for its own bottle. The
dining room, "Lounge of the Muses," was a depressing rackety
room of low ceilings and loud voices, in which the harried
Greek waiters slapped down course after course of inedibles,
followed by the hot-water drink labeled "coffee" and the

warm-water drink labeled "tea." The Powells had already established one corner of the lounge as their private gathering
place for drinks before and after dinner. No matter how foul
the food, you could always wash it away with strong brandy.

Whenever we landed, we ran for the nearest bar or market
or sidewalk café to stock up on provender, it didn't matter
what—a Breton cake, a baguette, a bottle of rum, Ricard, hard
cider, gin. If we were to be met by a bus for a sightseeing ex
cursion to some distinguished cathedral or castle, explicated by
our distinguished Oxford lecturer, inevitably the bus failed to
come or left us off at the wrong place or broke down or ran out
of gas.

We were an Erasmian Ship of Fools, characters who might
have been drawn by the satiric pen of a Powell or Amis in a
particularly vicious mood—the fat fish-lipped Vicar traveling
with a doddering Church Lady; the middle-aged Spinster Son in
raveled sweater traveling with his roly-poly Mum, whose bottom he had to push up the bus steps with his hands; the Siren,
who looked like a transvestite in her cowboy hat and pointy
bra; the Bête Noire who worried endlessly about exchange rates
and whether the Spanish would take Portuguese escudos; the
bright-eyed Ship's Doctor who told of two corpses they had to
put on ice during the last cruise and take off at night, because
people don't like deaths at sea; the Aussie Dwarf, a real one,
who turned out to be headmistress of a reputable American
girls' prep school; the Texan Couple with matching peroxide
hair, gold jewelry, and purple sunglasses; the white-bearded
Masseur with two Young Boys in tow like fishes on a line; the
Country Squire and Wife whose son was affianced to a Connecticut Divorcée whom they feared would not know what she
was in for, "marrying into a family of the distinction of the
Blofields of Blofield House"; and then there was the aristocratic

Lady Violet herself with her lavender voice and her watercolors and her Perfect Companion, Tony, constantly amused and amusing, with very large teeth and such exquisite manners that he would ask the ladies before eating an apple, "Do you mind if I bite?"

After the debacle of the banquet celebrating the Queen Mum's eightieth birthday (overcooked fish in lemon-water sauce, beef in brown gravy so tough that it could be neither cut nor chewed, a salad without dressing, ice cream with raspberry jam), I became somewhat more sympathetic to the Breakfast Lady, who had brought with her from England her own plastic tub of cooked oatmeal and a two-quart jar of homemade marmalade. She put up seventy or eighty pounds of marmalade a year, she said, but she and her husband ate less of it now than before the war, when they'd had high tea every night at six.

It was a relief to disembark in the Old Port at Nice, where we'd once embarked with the children on a converted P & O boat in January for an overnight trip to Corsica. The sea had been so wild and stormy that night that even if we'd not all been seasick, we'd have had to stick to our bunks anyway, because our cabin was awash in salt water. Now it was August, and we were late landing. All the hotels were booked and the tour agents, despite promises, had failed to find us a room. The Amises were taking a train that afternoon to Bordeaux, then to Paris and London, but we were to spend the night in Nice before flying home. We finally landed a suite at the Albert Premier that we couldn't afford. But at least the Amises could stash their many bags there while we had a last lunch. We ate omelettes and french fries and cheese and drank bottles of red wine at our old favorite outdoor snack bar, Queenie's, and were glad that the trip was over. None of us were sure what it had been for, but it was clear that more than the trip was over.

The scene at the train station in search of the Bordeaux Rapide was a final comedy of errors as we humped Kingsley's bags, bottles of booze clanking, from quai to quai until we located their carriage. Jane had said that morning as we slid past the ports of the Côte d'Azur how many happy memories she had of this particular coast. "You're lucky," Kingsley had said. "I have no happy memories." I was reminded of what Jane had said to me earlier when I'd excused some outrage by remarking, "You must remember we're not in England now." "Oh yes, we are," she'd replied. "We're always in England."

After they left, Paul and I took the long walk up to Chemin des Pins, looking for the Villa les Marguerites, but all the villas were gone, long replaced by massive high-rises with balconies, from one of which a pair of elderly women with dyed hair looked down at us with open hostility. Chez Puget, however, was still on rue Deloye, where Madame still rested her bosom on the cashier's podium. We reserved a table for dinner and walked along the Promenade des Anglais. The pebbled beach sported a number of topless girls sunning their breasts, another change. A row of elderly men watched silently from their deck chairs as a dark Niçois kissed passionately the breasts of a buxom blonde.

At Chez Puget that evening, the *soupe de poisson* was as excellent as before, topped with the same mustard-yellow *rouille*. The *poularde de Bresse en crème* was served with the same caramel sauce of old, and the squared roast potatoes and needle-thin *haricots verts* were still served on separate plates. We drank a costly Chablis, Grand Cru 1967. We lingered over our *cafés filtrés* and noted that the Puget son and daughter were not in evidence. All the waiters were old men, and Madame Puget did not recognize either our name or our faces. *Ce n'est plus pareil.*

That night, I found it impossible to sleep. Horns blared and sirens hee-hawed along the Baie des Anges. From the garden below the hotel, a rock concert was in full boom and, once it ended, freaked-out speedsters began to voice their hallucinations. I was still awake at dawn when a pale sun turned the sea powder blue and the moon, shaped like a croissant, faded behind an apron of rosy clouds.

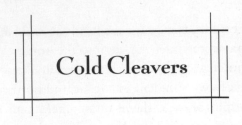

Cold Cleavers

LOBSTERS SEEMED TO PLAY a crucial role in the domestic crises of my life and perhaps that's why they are my favorite food. Should I find myself on Death Row, for a Last Meal I would probably request the lobster boiled or steamed. But the deepest sea flavor is in the shell, rather than in the tender, sweet, juicy, buttery flesh. The big advantage of lobster bisque, which begins with pulverized lobster shells, is that it offers up the deep-sea essence already distilled, requiring you to do no more than lift spoon to mouth.

The cook, however, must lift a cleaver. A single well-aimed blow severs chest from tail and brings a merciful and instantaneous death. Then, with a pair of serrated poultry shears, you cut open the chest in order to expose and save the strangely green and squishy liver—named "tomalley" by the natives of French Guiana and for no good reason the name stuck—and the lumpy black mess of eggs that fortunately turn pink when cooked and in English are appropriately named "coral." All these interior vitals, except for the head sac and ganglia and the long dark line of the intestine, go into the pot.

With your cleaver, you smash the legs and crack the claws, then flame them with the tail in cognac and butter and oil until they turn bright orange, then you simmer them in wine and herbs and a few chopped vegetables. The lobster meat you extract and save for garnish. It's the shells you want, and they go into a blender, to be pulverized coarsely before simmering in fish stock. Once you've strained out the shells, you add the tomalley and coral and any leaked lobster juices and smooth them out in the blender, and if you're like me you add quite a lot of heavy cream. As you savor your lobster bisque, spoonful by spoonful, you recite the mantra, "No omelettes without broken eggs, no bisques without decapitated lobsters."

I admit that this does not explain why, in 1980, I began to sleep with the cleaver under my pillow. But neither can I say just when the end began, which must mean there were many beginnings that made the end inevitable but kept it invisible. Did the end begin when I returned to graduate school at Rutgers in 1970? Did it begin in 1975, when Paul won a number of prestigious awards for his book on World War I, *The Great War and Modern Memory*, which catapulted him out of the narrow pigeon coop of English literature and onto the postwar cultural landscapes on both sides of the Atlantic? Or did it begin during our trip to India in 1977, when Paul returned to London because he'd had enough of a place he hated and I stayed on alone because I couldn't get enough of a place I loved? Certainly it had begun by the following year when for the first time I said no to a trip he wanted to take to Southeast Asia, not because I didn't want to go but because the timing meant I would have had to quit my job. And certainly it was a sure thing by the time I forced a family vacation on the four of us in 1980, trying to mend by a trip to Capri for our thirty-first wedding anniversary what soon broke down for good.

I went back to college the same decade Tucky and Sam graduated from college. In theory I now had time to do graduate work full-time, but in practice I knew that my full-time job was to take care of Paul, and anything else was moonlighting. There would be other problems. All my potential mentors at Rutgers were already friends. Worse, I was pushing my way into Paul's professional world, an amateur intent on turning pro. It made for some bizarre moments, particularly when I taught English at Rutgers for a couple of years while writing my thesis and sharing Paul's office. Rutgers was a bad idea all around, but Princeton took only full-time grad students and I knew that a daily commute to Columbia or NYU, even if they let me attend part-time, would be out of the question.

The real question was: what did I want a Ph.D. for? I thought it was because I didn't want to be a private first class for the rest of my life. Paul had confessed once that what he liked about the academy was that it was like the Army: the ranks were set and you worked your way up until you got to the top. No surprises as long as you obeyed the rules and kept your buttons polished. But you don't join the Army as a non-com at forty-five and expect to be a major at fifty, or even sixty, or at all. I told myself I needed the degree in order to get a permanent teaching job, but I wasn't scrutinizing either the job market or the sand in my hourglass. Secretly, I think I wanted validation for all those years spent as an academic wife with no identity tag of my own, no credit given and none taken. I wanted a Girl Scout merit badge for work well done.

Instead, Paul reaped the merit badges for his prize-winning book, and I faded like an old Polaroid. I grew resentful, but not, as Paul assumed, because I was jealous of his fame. I had wanted something simpler and subtler, some sign of recognition from him that his achievement, which was real and admirable, was the result of labor shared. The writing, the research, the sensibility, the work itself were all his, of course, but I had given him a gift he had used and discarded without thought. I had given him time. From the beginning I had freed him from all the secretarial and familial and social chores that unravel concentrated work, The Work. His work was my work, a trap I'd walked into as hungrily as a lobster with eyes on the baited prize. I'd walked in of my own volition, eager to support my mate with whole heart, like Dorothea her Casaubon, in *Middlemarch*, for the sake of *The Key to All Mythologies*.

But Dorotheas a century later were making new claims on time, their own and other people's, and new claims on education and work. The further they and other "minorities" invaded the universities, the more veterans like Paul stiffened their resistance. At home, we resumed our old gender debate full force. He no longer argued for the natural superiority of men—He for God only, she for God in him—but rather for the order of merit: To the worthy go the spoils—and somehow the worthy were always male.

Naturally Paul's resistance fired my determination to win some prize, however meager, in the only game he valued, the only game I knew how to play. But returning to boring lectures and interminable reading lists and footnoted papers was like sitting down to leftovers of a meal I'd begun twenty years earlier. I fell asleep rereading *The Faerie Queene*, which had once upon a time kept me up all night. I chafed under instructors half my age, or so ancient they were doddering, or under ex-hippie types who smoked pot with pet students and played games of psychological manipulation. And the truth was I still could not write a clear and logical expository essay. I was

working against the grain of my thinking, which was not se-
quential, and my desire, which was to imitate the works I read,
not analyze them.

Once I had my prize, the kind you can hang on your office
wall, I had no office, and no job. Rutgers was done with part-
time instruction. I sent out dozens of letters to nearby institutions offering my services, but got only one reply, by phone. I
was out at the time, and when the caller asked if I would be
available to teach a Shakespeare course, Paul explained that we
were going to spend the fall semester in London. He forgot all
about the call until the next day, when he mentioned it offhand-
edly. If I really wanted to teach more than anything, it was clear
I'd have to leave Paul. But still I chose to stay.

This time our London apartment was owned by a corporation in Yemen that had rented it before it was finished, as if it
ever would be. It was without heat and without furniture, save
a minimal stove, and so badly constructed that when I went to
open a window one day the entire frame came out in my hands
and I had to holler for help to keep it and me from falling to
the sidewalk below and smashing into a thousand pieces.

I was glad to escape in November to India, which I had always longed to see. Paul was appalled by everything there was
to be appalled by, the filth, noise, stench, beggars, cows, cobras,
cripples, dung, corpses, chaos. The strangeness that made him
want to flee enthralled me. Most of my time was spent trying to
get tickets from one place to the next no matter what it took,
and it took a very great deal of time and patience and elbow-
ing, but the sensuous overkill of the place was as exhilarating
as my first discovery of the sensuality of food. I couldn't believe
our luck at arriving in Calcutta during the Feast of Kali. We
watched as a priest sacrificed a goat before a temple and wor-
shippers bathed in its blood. God in the streets! Paul cut his trip

short, and I stayed on by myself, traveling through southern India by train, shuffling into dark temples with thousands of redolent bodies to crowd against a primeval stone lingam in the blackness.

Back in the States, I began to pursue a different line of work. I'd done some research on the life of the silent screen comedienne Mabel Normand, but it was proceeding slowly. In the meantime, I was starting to write articles about food. *The New York Times* had just transformed the "Woman's Page" into "The Living Section," in an attempt to embrace both sexes and a swelling interest in food and the kitchen. My first piece for them was on the history of Jell-O.

I'd been trained in the pompous jargon of the academy, and I had a tough time retraining myself to write the way people actually spoke. I tackled each project as if I were composing a 750-page book, not a 750-word article. I would acquire far too much information and then agonize over what to select and how to shape it. It began to dawn on me that the reason I had so much trouble writing essays was that I had no faith in my own judgment as to what was important and what was not. And thanks to my live-in critic, I was never going to develop any. I knew I had to find a space away from Paul, some kind of room of my own, if I were to be anything more than a handmaid to his writing, his career, his fame.

Naturally, this made me the Enemy. I had read and reread his book in manuscript and had made comments his editor later echoed. I had assured him it was the best thing he'd ever written, but none of that seemed to penetrate. En route to Mexico to spend New Year's with friends who had retired to Chiapas, Paul developed an abscessed tooth. It was so agonizingly painful that while we waited for our friends to arrive back from the airport where we'd somehow missed each other, Paul drank the entire bottle of Wild Turkey we'd brought for our hosts. It did not ease his pain, but it uncorked emotion, as did the dose of Seconal our host, a retired doctor, gave him to knock him out. "Not once did she say, 'Good work, Paul, job well done,' " he railed. "She didn't even read the fucking book once it was out." By now it was long past midnight, and when Paul finally stood up, he fell straight over, in mid-sentence, like an axed tree. We dragged him into bed, where he slept the night away, but I couldn't sleep. I was dumbstruck at the anger he'd been harboring toward me, at the monster he saw in me.

I got a job teaching Comedy at the New School in New York one day a week. A friend who'd be away for a semester was willing to sublet her railroad apartment on Ninety-first and Lexington, so that I'd have a place to prepare my class and continue my research on Mabel. Paul couldn't understand why I didn't rent an office in Princeton. Then I could write during the day and come home each night. And of course pick up groceries on the way home and cook them up and have a few friends over for drinks and get into knockdown fights disguised as intellectual discussions and stay up late complaining about everybody after they'd gone—the usual routine. He couldn't understand that if I didn't break the routine, the routine would break me. I yearned to create something permanent, something concrete, to have something to show at the end of a few decades' hard work. Instead of making a loaf of bread that might keep for a week, I wanted to make a book that would last for years. I wanted a longer shelf life.

To write I would have to remove myself from the very air that surrounded Paul and me, echoing with our eternal duet. "You can't write," he'd say. "Why don't you do something you're good at?" "Like what?" she'd say. "Cooking," he'd say. And she heard but didn't heed and struggled to put words and sentences together on a piece of paper for the same reason she put artichokes and lamb together on a plate. And she continued to show him her work because he had skills she lacked, and if he hacked the writing to pieces, she deserved what she got: confirmation that writing was his job, and all she was good for was to cook. She saw what had compelled a generation of daughters to slam the kitchen door and proudly announce that they knew how to be doctors and lawyers and bankers but they did not know and did not want to know how to cook.

I was unraveling fast. Paul had begun to exercise what he called "selective deafness." The moment I opened my mouth I could feel him turn off his mental hearing aid and tune me out. It made me so jittery that I found myself stuttering, or saying "heartfelt" when I meant to say "handmade," or "Freud" when I meant "Einstein."

I went manic. I would wake in the middle of the night, my head bursting with ideas, and run down to the library, where I pulled books from the shelves at random—Erasmus's *In Praise of Folly* or Powdermaker's *Hollywood, the Dream Factory*—and read avidly for two or three hours and felt lightbulbs exploding all over the place, and then I went back to bed and didn't remember anything I'd read when I woke up.

I began to cry again, the way I'd cried in my childhood. The tears would come out of nowhere, and I couldn't stop them. Crying was just one of the things I did, like sneezing from permanent hay fever. I would look in the bathroom mirror and see an image as distant and remote as Paul's.

I found I could no longer stomach academic gamesmanship, in which anger was disguised as argument. The underlying aggression was too palpable, the need to dominate too naked to ignore. Was Samuel Beckett a serious artist or a put-on? Was or was not folk art a contradiction in terms? *Help*, said a still small voice inside me. "Discourse" had become a favorite cant term of the deconstructionists, but to me all conversations were imploding, all words seemed empty and pompous. In the heat of a debate, I who was as smilingly polite as a Japanese wife heard myself say to a longtime friend, "You're full of shit." He didn't speak to me for a year and I was glad, because words were superfluous. One day during a lengthy argument with Paul over the relative aesthetic value of film versus literature, Sam asked me quietly, "When are you and Dad going to get a divorce?" The question shocked me. "It's all talk, my dear," I told him. "We just argue to exercise our jaws."

Still, even I could see that I was not in good shape. Desperate to find out what was wrong, why I was crying, why I was manic, why I felt I was losing my mind, and—good Presbyterian that I was—to do something about it, I had asked Paul's permission to find a shrink in New York, because he was the one who would have to foot the bill. Presbyterians didn't go to shrinks, they had God to talk to. But God wasn't taking my calls these days, and I had nowhere else to go. By great luck I found the woman I called the Shrinkess, a young mother half my age. I gave her a piece I was writing for the *Times* on fake food, like the plastic sushi models you saw in the windows of Japanese restaurants. "Your mind and body are on separate tracks," she said. "Just tell me how you feel about it. Just tell me what you see." I had to be told that what I felt, what I saw, mattered. I had to clear my throat and find a voice at last.

By this time I'd been given a regular column of restaurant reviews for the New Jersey section of the Sunday *New York Times*. My editor thought she was doing me a favor. She had never lived in New Jersey. The Manhattan reviewer, who had never lived in New Jersey either, had insisted that Manhattan standards be applied to the suburbs in order not to dilute the value of the rating. According to the rules, you had to visit each place twice, retain total anonymity, and sample as much of the menu as possible. Paul had said at the beginning, "Count me out," which meant I had to rely on the kindness of friends to get mouths for hundreds of meals all over the state. But while I hated the threatening letters and telephone calls from outraged diners and chefs to whom anything less than a three-star puff was an insult, I liked seeing my name in print. I also liked the instant feedback from friends who'd been entertained by my prose, even if Paul's highest praise was "cute."

Not until I found a restaurant that I thought a potential four-star did I ask Paul to go with me on the second visit. As usual, the restaurant was hell to get to and Paul was not in good humor by the time we did. His mood did not improve with the first course. His objections grew louder and nastier as the meal went on and finally became so vehement that the couple next to us, who were actually enjoying their meal, turned and asked what we had ordered that was so awful. On the drive back I was angry, not because Paul hadn't enjoyed his meal but because he was determined that I knock the place down to one or two stars at the most. When I objected, he said, "What did you want me along for if you didn't value my opinion?" He could not accept that in this one insignificant arena, it was my opinion, and only mine, that mattered.

When Paul announced that he was going to take a trip to visit war sites in Hawaii, Japan, and major islands of the South Pacific, he couldn't believe that I didn't want to go with him. Travel had always brought us together, just as living at home had always pulled us apart. But I knew that if I quit this job to fit myself into his agenda, I'd never have a job.

It was around this time that Paul became obsessed with his body. He took to wearing nylon bikini briefs in Day-Glo colors that he ordered from catalogues. He became fanatic about his Canadian Army isometric exercises, this man for whom croquet was heavy exercise. I knew he was terrified of regressing to the Fat Boy of his youth, but there was something more. When I stayed up talking with friends late into the night it wasn't unusual for Paul to descend the stairs nude and parade about the room until someone said, "Oh, Paul, go back to bed." But now I would find, when I came to bed, that he'd shaved off all his pubic hair. "I was drunk," he'd say next morning when I asked why. I could feel fantasies thick as bedcovers over us, but he would not talk about them or even admit he had any. Sex was not something you talked about. It was something you did, alone or with somebody else.

He took a trip to Russia with a handful of prominent scholars, as part of an official cultural exchange. When he came back, he couldn't stop talking about a student he'd met, a boy to whom he'd promised to send a pair of expensive leather cowboy boots. Some days I returned from New York to find him stretched on the library couch listening to records of Russian music. Did it matter, I wondered, if he had a crush on a young Russian boy? When a friend who knew one of the professors on the trip told him she was a pal of Paul's wife, the man was incredulous. "You mean to tell me that guy's married?" Paul took to singing the praises of a student whom he'd had to dinner more than once when I was in New York and mentioned that they'd exchanged jackets. Exchanged jackets? Sure enough, there in his closet instead of his expensive Harris tweed was tattered denim.

Even our entertaining life took an odd turn. On our honeymoon, Paul had fantasized blowing up the bridge that con-

nected Cape Cod to the mainland, and declaring himself King
of the Cape. When we were in India, he'd bought a sackful of
colorful zircons and topazes, which we jokingly called his
Crown Jewels. A friend who was a jeweler fashioned a crown
out of scrap metal, inserting the jewels between "rubies" of bi-
cycle reflector buttons. I dug out a Charles II black wig with
black curls and stitched up a cape with fake ermine. On our
terrace, we staged the formal investiture of the Duke of Raritan, and his Duchess served an enormous banquet to honor his
court—the Royal Jeweler, the Royal Archivist, the Keeper of
the Keys, everyone got into the act. But were we playing Jarry's
Ubu Roi or Pirandello's *Henry IV*? And was I the Duchess of
Raritan or the Fool?

If home life was weirdly like a pantomime, New York was
scary because it was too real. The bedroom in the apartment I'd
rented had a window that opened onto the back fire escape.
Just before my sublet began, there'd been a break-in, and my
friend had installed an iron gate with a big padlock on it. If I
wanted air, I had to unlock the gate, heave the window up,
prop it open with a stick, close the gate, and lock it. But I was
unused to city sounds and sights. The window looked across
the court into a brightly lit apartment where a man with black
sideburns hit his blond companion across the chops with the
back of his hand. Or was I only imagining it, making a Hitch-
cock movie out of an ordinary domestic spat? I watched them
in the dark, like Jimmy Stewart, fascinated by domestic violence that was so open.

I undressed in the dark, so that no one would know I was in
the apartment. As I lay in bed and listened to the sirens wail, I
wondered what I was doing there when I could have been lying
safe in my bed in Princeton. But for the first time, I was learning to think for myself, without fear of contempt or contumely.

I could think any way I wanted, say anything I wanted. It was as if I'd picked up my life where I'd left it when I'd first come to New York. I was on my own.

When the sublet was up I found another one, this one in the Village, in a building owned by the neighboring Episcopal Church. The apartment belonged to an Anglo-American woman, a writer, who was going to spend a few months in London deciding whether or not to marry the Englishman she'd taken up with. The problem was, she was not just eccentric but disturbed. When I opened the door to her apartment for the first time, a Siamese cat sprang at me howling. The woman had left it there for four days without food. It turned out I'd inherited not only the starving cat but a history of hostility between her and the church and between her and her downstairs neighbor. He would telephone me in the middle of the night when I was sleeping and shout that my noise was keeping him awake. He finally took his paranoia and his grievances to the rector, accusing my subletter and me of being professional prostitutes who were blaspheming the church. The rector forthwith kicked me out. It was an odd moment for a suburban matron trying to start a new life. Later I learned that my landlady had killed herself in England.

I tried to carry on as usual in Princeton, but my old life no longer had much life in it. Entertaining had become a burden, and I did it less and less. Paul was always dieting, so our daily fare was sparse and dull. When he decided to entertain the entire English Department and their spouses to honor a retiring secretary, I sank to a new low: I ordered fried chicken and potato salad from a local deli. One spouse was overheard to say, "She's supposed to be such a great cook and this is the crap she serves?"

By this time I was sleeping with the cleaver under my pillow.

It was a crude Chinese cleaver, about a foot long, with a wooden handle and a blade so thick no amount of sharpening would give it an edge, but fine chopping was not what it was about. It was about heft, and it could halve a chicken in a single blow. A friend had given it to me because she said she never used it. She liked to serve a roast chicken whole, and she used her chef's knife for chopping vegetables. Besides hacking through bones, her cleaver could also smash garlic or anything else that got in your way, but during the period it did time under my pillow, I didn't miss it in the kitchen at all.

Paul was often away on some lecture tour or other, and I lay awake and alone in the dark, cut by a slice of moonlight through the window by my bed as I waited for sleep that was long in coming. When I heard a creak upon the stairs, an odd thump in the dark as one or another of our cats leaped and landed, the scenario would begin to play. The intruder had come in through the French windows of the dining room and perhaps paused for a handful of peanuts from a kitchen counter before he made for the staircase. At the top, he could turn right into Tucky's bedroom, but he would soon see that it was empty of anything more valuable than a Chagall print and a Who poster.

Or he could turn left and move down the narrow corridor to the master bedroom, attracted by a glint of mirror on the vanity, in the drawer of which lay a dazzling assortment of costume jewelry that even in the dark he would not mistake for real. A small Persian rug was the only thing of value, but that he would not know even in the light. There was never any money in the house, but he would not know that either.

The intruder would enter my bedroom through the door on my right and pass by the head of my bed, which faced the fireplace beyond. At an earlier time, when my fears were less definite, I had imagined using the poker to defend myself, but now I recognized that it would be difficult to get to and awkward to wield. No, a cleaver was simpler, cleaner, easier to grab, and packed more of a wallop. Not that the intruder had entered with rape on his mind but, having found nothing more than a drawerful of silver and a handful of cheap beads for his trouble, he might feel that a warm female body offered some redemption of an otherwise lost night.

Unfortunately, the very ordinariness of the farmhouse in Capote's *In Cold Blood* had made a strong impression on my middle years, confirming every *True Detective* story I had read as a child by flashlight under the covers, reveling in the forbidden, hair-raising pages of black-and-white photos showing bloodied bodies and smashed heads. For me, the house had never been a sure Place, the body never inviolable, innocence never the first defense.

Even now I had my escape route mapped out in the same detail with which I'd elaborated my flight from the house on Walnut Street in the event the Japs landed. Forty years had not changed the basic plan. Once I heard the footsteps of the intruder approaching the bedroom, I would slip silently from the bed and exit through the bathroom and on through the study to another hallway beyond, then down a back stairway and out through the garage to the front yard, or out the back door and across the backyard into my neighbor's yard, and finally into the street, which would of course be empty, as would all the adjoining streets, and in the wee hours no one would be mad enough to respond to a crazy woman in a nightie banging on a door.

Unless he got to you first. Let's say he was in the room before you were aware, and all you could do was pretend to be asleep. Let's say you hadn't heard him at all until he was on top of you, as had happened to the daughter of a friend of ours, who woke to feel a man's hairy balls dangling in her face. She was a smart, cool girl who later became a psychiatrist in the U.S. Army and revealed at this moment her future capacities by talking the guy into telling his story instead of doing anything further with his balls. But let's say he didn't feel like talking. That's where a cleaver would come in handy, provided you could get one hand free to grasp the handle and aim for the neck.

The Shrinkess laughed at my cleaver. We had taken to exchanging recipes and we talked a lot about food. She liked recipes to be exact and followed them exactly. She was a scientist, I was an improviser, but we found common emotional ground in kitchen talk. In the course of our conversations, she changed my diagnosis from "depressive with tendency to martyrdom" to "exacerbated environment." I rolled the syllables of "exacerbated environment" on my tongue with the delight of Holofernes in *Love's Labour's Lost*, relishing the labials of "remuneration."

Exactly why I kept a cleaver beneath my pillow may have been clear to the Shrinkess from the start, but it didn't become clear to me until the end. It began with another routine affair, the Professor's annual student beer bust at the end of spring term. Food was there largely to sop up the beer, boy food like cold meats and store-bought breads laid out on trays with mustard and mayonnaise and pickles, along with potato salad, cole slaw, popcorn, peanuts, pretzels, potato chips, corn chips, and the obligatory gesture toward health in raw carrots and celery. Prole food, the Professor liked to call it, and he loved every bite.

I loved it less and, over the years, made an ever-shorter appearance among boys who were certainly not there to meet a
prof's wife, but who were happy to play Frisbee in the backyard and listen to jazz turned up high on the stereo and, as the
evening progressed, to crash into furniture and occasionally
throw up on the lawn. I was happy to do my obligatory once-
around handshake, make a bologna sandwich, and retire to the
bedroom with a glass of beer. The problem was noise. I could
read until the cows came home but I couldn't go to sleep until
the boys went home.

This party was a particularly raucous one. It had begun
around four in the afternoon and by midnight riffs of life still
wafted up from downstairs, but at least the sound was now
concentrated in the library. Then there were noisy farewells and
the zoom of motors along our lane. Finally we were down to
soft music and hushed voices, but it was now around two in the
morning and it was certainly time for all boys to be gone. I
thought perhaps an appearance in my bathrobe would provide
the necessary hint. But the door to the library was closed, and
the voices were low. I got a glass of seltzer, went back upstairs,
and tried to read. It was now after three and quiet below, but
where was the Professor? Fears that clutch your stomach I was
used to, but this was not fear of an unknown intruder creeping
up the stairs. Instead, it was I creeping down the stairs, and my
fear was of what I might find.

The door was closed. The lights were out. It was quiet. I
went into the kitchen and turned on the light, a signal that
someone was up and about. I got another glass of seltzer and
slammed the refrigerator door. Another signal, if anyone
wanted to hear. I stood in the middle of the kitchen and considered my choices. I could turn out the light, go back upstairs, and pretend to go to sleep, as if nothing was amiss. Or I

could turn on the light in the study and confront a truth long denied.

I turned out the kitchen light. I paused outside the study door because I knew this was a Pandora's box that once opened I could never shut. Then I opened the door and turned on the light. There were the Professor and the Student, buck naked, as startled as a pair of deer caught in headlights. The Professor tried drunkenly to explain that it had been too late for the Student to get a bus home, so he was going to spend the night on the living-room sofa. I told the boys to put on their clothes, told the Professor to go to bed, and told the Student I'd drive him home. I must have looked like an angry Housemother confronting bad behavior in the dorm, but to myself I was Madame Defarge before the guillotine.

It took three-quarters of an hour, even with deserted roads, to get the Student back to his dorm in New Brunswick, so we had time for conversation. As in: "You know, Mrs. Fussell, you'd feel a lot better if you just told me how you feel." As in: "I hope you realize, Mrs. Fussell, this has absolutely nothing to do with you." I noted that he was not as drunk as the Professor, because he could get through a word like "absolutely" without slurring. I was a paradigm of cool, like the iceberg the *Titanic* hit. I found out where he'd come from, how he was studying to be an engineer but thought maybe he'd like to be a poet. I kept him talking and dropped him—"Yeah, if you'd just hang a right here"—in front of his dorm so he could say, "Take care, now."

And then I drove back the way I came, on Route 27, a road I'd driven for nearly thirty years, while acting, while teaching, while getting my Ph.D., while ferrying Sam to soccer practice and Tucky to piano lessons. I'd driven it to friends' houses sober and driven it home drunk, driven it to meet my lover in a

poison ivy patch. Twice I'd been driven down it, to the hospital
to deliver babies. I could feel my heart pumping to the rhythm
of the tires and my teeth slammed tight in my jaw.

When I got home, I made another bologna sandwich in the
kitchen, filled up another glass of beer, went upstairs and sat in
the blue leather chair in the Professor's study, and read. I read a
recent book of literary essays because I knew it would focus
what was left of my mind. I could feel my heart behind my left
breast, frozen and cracked. I didn't know how it could keep on
pumping. I read the book from first page to last, including ac-
knowledgments and index, which took me until nine in the
morning, when Paul had to get up, hungover or no, to receive
the university's Teacher of the Year Award at a luncheon for
students and their parents.

When I went to make the bed, after he'd dressed and shaved
and gone, I took the cleaver and put it back in the knife block
in the kitchen. The things that go bump in the night had been
given a name and a shape at last, and maybe not the right
name, but at least I knew that what scared me was not something I'd made up inside some dark psychotic recess of my own.
It was out there, it was real, tangible, a happening that divided
before and after in one clean stroke. There would be no more
tears, no more fear of drowning, no more shouldering alone the
backpack of guilt for everything that went wrong with our
journey. From now on we would go separately. The truth had
divided us, but the truth had made me free.

The next time I took up the cleaver was almost a year later,
long after Paul had gone to England and returned to live in an
apartment in the middle of town. I was in the kitchen, cutting
up live lobsters to test out a recipe for lobster bisque for my

first cookbook. In it I wanted to explain how I'd learned to cook from books, from American books written by the masterful quartet of Claiborne, Child, Beard, and Fisher. I'd gotten a contract with one publisher the day after I learned that my Mabel manuscript had been accepted by another, about a week after my night of truth. On both days we were having lunch. Paul's response to the Mabel contract was to break open a bottle of champagne and then suddenly stop. "My God, I'd better get upstairs and get cracking." His response to the second book lacked champagne. "Anyone can write a cookbook. Why didn't you do it sooner?"

In the week that followed, Paul made many decisions, often within the same week, sometimes within the same day. We should stay married, and he'd give up alcohol. We should split and live however we wanted for a while, have a lot of sexual partners, see how it went. We should get a divorce; he'd talked to his lawyer. Sex had nothing to do with it.

That summer was unreal, with Tucky taking courses at Pratt and Sam renting an apartment in New York, and Paul and me trying to make bisque out of the carcass of our marriage. For the first time, I left my marital bed to sleep in Tucky's room, and Paul was hurt. We came together at mealtimes, in the kitchen. Cooking and eating were the last rituals left us, and neither of us wanted to dismantle them. We would drift down to the kitchen from our separate studies and our separate typewriters and open a bottle of house wine. Paul thought white wine less caloric than red, so we would fill our glasses with ice cubes and pour on the Frascati or the Bolla Soave and I would fix something simple like steak and salad and we would for the first and only time in our married life talk straight, because there was no other way to talk.

We talked about our mutual sexual betrayals. When it came

to naming names, I was no less surprised than he. "Not Chessie
Franklin, she was so ugly," I'd say. "She had a huge crush on
me," he'd say. "I knew she wanted me, so we went up to the
bedroom and had half an hour between courses." To my surprise, he hadn't known about my affair with Dave. Of the
crowning incident, he'd say, "This would never have happened
if I hadn't been so lonely." "But you just admitted you're inca-
pable of loving anyone but yourself," I'd say. "Well, you would
have distracted me," he'd say. "From *what*," I'd say, "yourself?" "Precisely," he'd say. "I don't want to live with a man, I
want to live with a woman. I like the opposition. I'm aggres-
sive, you're recessive."

The talk was not always this polite, particularly as the bottle neared its end. Paul just wanted to contemplate youth and
beauty—to touch, to kiss, he said, but not to sodomize. That
was repulsive, "putting your cock in shit." When I suggested he
might try a shrink, he objected mightily. "I don't want to
change," he'd say. "I've built my whole life on a set of intellectual principles, how can I change that?" It was all my fault.
"You never wanted sex," he'd say. "I always had to ask." "You
used sex like a weapon to keep me in my place," I'd say. "You
were making war, not love."

When I said that I knew he didn't find a woman's body
beautiful, he'd say, "Someone would have to convince me that
Bronzino's *Portrait of a Boy* is not the most beautiful thing I
have ever seen." He'd kept a small bronze statue of Donatello's
David on his desk, but I'd never made the connection. He'd say
I was out to punish him for a mere peccadillo out of professional jealousy. "You want to do the one thing you have no talent for, if I may speak bluntly," he'd say. "Frankly, I wanted to
save you from embarrassing yourself in public with your jour-
nalism. You have no talent for language, but you admire it be-

cause you're around literary people." "And what *do* I have talent for?" I'd ask, knowing his answer but wondering if he'd still have the nerve. He did. "Cooking, I suppose, and whatever it involves—presentation, patience, painstaking detail."

My husband too had his terrors in that house. I came home one night from New York to find him deeply upset. "One of my enemies has gotten in and shit in the sheets." What? "I pulled back the sheet to get into bed and there were two horrible black blobs," he said, "so I ripped the sheets off the bed and put a chair up against the bedroom doors." Where was the cat? "She was in the study and bedroom with the doors shut because the air conditioning was on," he said, "but this was no excreta from a cat." I went down to look at the sheets in the washing machine, where he'd dumped them, and found without surprise that the blobs were cat shit.

After we separated, he finally went to see a shrink for a few weeks, just long enough to discover, as he related with disbelief, that he'd always connected sex with shame, with dirtiness, which he'd gotten from his mother—of course. A mastoid operation as an adolescent had kept him home for six months and he'd become a mama's boy, learning to knit and sew while his older brother went out for sports and girls. "The shrink says I'm a permanent adolescent," he said. "I never grew up and that's what makes getting old such a shock. Adolescents aren't supposed to be old." He was attracted to students who were straight, he said, because he got a charge from their youth. "I don't want to be with old people like me."

Change was not in the cards for him, but it was my turn to deal, and I was changing fast. I wanted to be as old as my years and as old as the experience that filled them. I wanted to deny neither body nor mind. I knew I could put words together, if I worked at it, just as I could put ingredients together on a plate.

Patience at the typewriter was surely as important as patience at the stove, and painstaking detail was what any art was about. Although I had seen many things in nature and in art as beautiful as Bronzino's boy, I was not hooked on youth or boys. I was hooked on the wondrous changes that turn boys into men and girls into women and kittens into cats and the raw materials of nature into the creative ferment of art.

No change without breakage, and the biggest change for the four of us was breaking up the house. Paul had sold it to friends while I was off in California, but I had a full year in which to adjust, to sell the books and furniture, to put things into storage that I couldn't bear to part with, to shuttle back and forth between the study and the kitchen to test out recipes for the cookbook and write them up. I wrote and cooked and cooked and wrote in a frenzy, completing a massive book within the year because I knew I would never again have such a kitchen at my command and never again have such a fierce need to prove that I could write as well as cook.

Meanwhile, negotiations on the house moved slowly after the initial contract. First there was termite inspection, and I had to bring in the exterminators. Then there was elm blight inspection, because we still had a few remaining elms in the yard thanks to assiduous spraying. Our real estate agent was a close friend, as were the buyers, but that only made each of their intrusions worse, made them personal.

So there I was with cleaver in hand on an April afternoon, trying to deal with a pair of live lobsters on the chopping block, when the friend who had bought our house stopped by to ask if she could bring her gardener around to inspect the shrubbery and plantings. I didn't know how much I minded losing the house until I heard myself yelling at her, "If you don't want the house, say so. If you do, get out of my kitchen." And with that,

I held the body of the lobster firmly, and as it tried to curl its tail under and wave its rubber-banded claws in the air for help, I severed its thick carapace at the vital spot between head and tail, ending at once life, motion, and talk.

The thing about lobsters is how slowly they grow. It may take a lobster seven years to weigh as much as a pound, and I usually prefer big boys who weigh two. Lobstermen trap them in a wood-slatted box that has two compartments, the "parlor" in front and the "kitchen" behind. That's what they call them. The kitchen is where the action is, because there lies the bait, like a delicious little crab that the hungry lobster heads for when he enters the parlor. Once in, he can't turn around or back out, but at least he has a Last Meal of crab.

As a chef I know says, with a lobster you've got a primitive face-off, one on one, first with the fisherman, then with the cook, then with the eater. Maybe that's why I go for lobsters. All I know is that when I taste one, I taste first my honeymoon on Cape Cod and then the lobster dinners at the Griswold Inn in New London, the flavor intensified by all those intervening years and sorrows and angers and fears, which great Neptune's ocean cannot wash clean because the sea is as full of salt as of other things and when you ope your legs to the sea you embrace not just your dreams but all that is.

Breaking and Entering
with a Wooden Spoon

ONE JUNE EVENING of the following year, when the last rays of sun slanted across the tiles, my daughter and I stood in the middle of the kitchen and opened our second bottle of champagne. The bottle and two paper cups were all that remained. The accumulated nestings of four lives had been vomited up and wiped clean by auction, book sale, garage sale, Salvation Army, and Goodwill, until finally a hired truck hauled away to a dump the junk not even the cleaning lady or the junk man would take. The kitchen without chairs or tables or stools or hanging pots and pans was discomfiting, but not creepy like the rest of the house. The terracotta tiles kept their glow, the stainless steel its shine. One drawer even kept until this moment—"Hey, Mom, look what I found"—a simple wooden spoon, shaped from olive wood, bought in Arles and never used because I'd tucked it away to give as a present and it had remained hidden in the dark.

The kitchen pulsed with life that made the rest of the rooms seem forlorn. We walked through them with our bottle and cups, toasting the wall above the living-room mantel streaked with smoke, the replastered spot where the ceiling had leaked, the black-painted hardwood floors that, stripped of rugs, had not looked so clean since they were sanded and painted and re-sanded and repainted, after the painters had got it wrong and put on a coat of glossy black instead of matte, and there was much complaint on all sides, but this was the house we were going to go out of feet first and we wanted it to be exactly as we wanted it before we went.

Tucky was a much better tosser-out than I and a much bet-ter goer. "I hated this house," she said. "We were never a fam-ily here." For me each toss was like losing a finger or toe. I was woven into the fabric of the rugs, no matter how worn. I was glued into the rungs of the small Victorian settee I had mended and covered in bottle-green velvet when its horsehair seat tore. I was stripped, stained, and urethaned into the round walnut dining table that was split through the middle so that you could lay in four warped leaves, transforming an intimate circle into an oval arena. I was buried in each of the dozen earthenware pots, along with the roots of the six-foot avocado trees I'd started from pits that had balanced on toothpicks in jars of wa-ter until the force of the green germ split them in two. Each ob-ject had sprouted its own history long before it had become part of mine—had been chosen *because* of its history of human hands shaping wool, wood, horsehair, or leather, as if sowing what later hands would tend and cherish.

Cherished objects, like images, as the modern philosophe Gaston Bachelard tells us, have a life of their own, which we become part of when they become part of us. I could tour every room of the house and recall which piece of trash and which genuine antique, cherished alike, came from where, and when. I remembered the auction at which I had acquired the turquoise-and-beige Kazak rug, bigger than anyone else wanted, lucky for us. The extendable table came from a two-story warehouse of Victorian junk in New Brunswick when Victoriana could be had for a player-piano song. The settee we'd gotten at a New Jersey farm near Ringoes, where an old woman sat rocking on the porch that was auctioned out from under her as she watched the current of her life seep into the hands of strangers. I had seen another woman cry when her set of imitation Chippendale chairs—the pride of a dining-room suite lovingly dusted over the years, as children waxed and grown-ups waned, until even the kitchen was too big to eat in—was sold for twenty-five dollars for the lot. I knew that my pleasure in these bargains was purchased at the cost of someone else's pain, and that part of the price was the responsibility for cherishing the object of someone else's affections.

Our garage sale had been a joke. How much for mended teacups? What price for the Mickey Mouse phone I'd bought for Paul one Christmas, which I valued more than the antique washstand in which we'd housed our first record player? And how could I sell at all the white organdy cocktail-length dress with tulle veil and fake orange-blossom wreath and fingerless lace gloves I'd gotten married in? I couldn't just chuck them all and begin anew as Paul had done, priding himself on a clean start the way I imagine my Scotch-Irish forebears had done when they chucked a cow and a sheep and took off for Iowa, while their women agonized over leaving behind that one piece of good linen with the tatted edging that worked the past into the present and gave both meaning.

Yet I knew also that the most cherished object must, sometimes, be sacrificed. Once a year, I'm told, the few remaining

Lacandón Indians of the Chiapas rain forest break their god pots and stamp out their hearth fires, as Maya descendants have done for two thousand years, in order to begin the year anew. One of these god pots sits in my living room now on a table crowded with other sacred objects—a ceramic pre-Columbian corn god, a bottle of sand from the Sahara, a silver-lined bowl for yak butter offerings from Tibet. The god pot is the most powerful of these Penates because it is the ugliest. Its body is a crudely shaped bowl of clay attached to a head with a square face, open mouth, and protruding lower lip. Its mouth, filled with clay pebbles, mirrors the bowl, which the Lacandón fill with chunks of resinous copal, to burn as incense before they smash the pot.

The books were hardest to sacrifice. I was packing up my lives, both spent and unspent, when I attacked the shelves to divest them of our five thousand–odd volumes. As much as pots and pans, books were my sandbags, my bulwark against the dark, not just for their contents but for their corporeal selves. For years, we'd simplified moving by using stacked wooden apple crates as bookcases. At moving time, the books were already boxed, and we had only to restack them and repaint. But this was the house where we'd finally discarded our crates for built-in bookcases, because we were never going to move again. They lined our rooms like a double-thick fortress wall.

It was like fleeing a house on fire. What did you grab to save, and what did you consign to the flames? Hardest to burn were the shelves of Shakespearean criticism from my days and nights at Harvard, desperately catching up. Kittredge, Boas, Brooke, Stauffer, Tillyard, Dowden, Stoll, the names like bells tolling the death of my scholarship. I looked at my penciled underlinings and annotations, the exclamation marks, the expletives, the condescending "good point," the arrogant "fatuous."

I could smell again, like discharged lightning, the excitement of that time. But I would never read these books again. I was through with the academy.

Out went the works in Latin and Greek, my copy of the *Iliad* marred by arrows pointing to adjectives modifying precedent nouns. Out went the works of the greats, which you could always find in the library—Austen, Dickens, Conrad, James, Faulkner, Hemingway, Dostoevsky, acquired one by one in Everyman or Modern Library until you had them all, each a monument of discovery recorded by the date in the upper right-hand corner of the flyleaf. Tucky had gone through the shelves to pick out what she wanted, but where was she going to put books in her one-room apartment in New York? Sam, who at this moment was immersed in modern greats at Oxford, wasn't there to choose, so we put together a solid arts-and-letters library for when he got back home where there was no home.

I was dispersing my children's lives as well as my own. I packed for each a trunk of memorabilia, drawings from kindergarten, misshapen clay ashtrays, essays marked with "A," Tucky's peasant dress and cap from Heidelberg at age three, Sam's first catcher's glove at six, miniature Steiff animals, Matchbox cars, horse-show ribbons, soccer trophies. But G.I. Joe and his equipage would have to go, and the boxes of neon-haired gremlins. Maybe there was room in Sam's trunk for one of his hobby-kit Godzilla monsters, as there had to be room in Tucky's for her tiny hand-drawn books of cartoons held together by straight pins.

Paul had finally left in October to work for two months at the British War Museum in London, arranging for whatever books, furniture, and pictures he wanted to be moved into an apartment a few blocks from our house on his return. I made sure to be out of the house when he moved. I had no words left to say goodbye to all that, or to him. From New York I'd written, "You're breaking my heart," a wimpy cliché that was physically true. How else to explain the deep chest pain that felt as if some connective tissue was tearing or some interior vessel shattering? His reply was an index card left on the kitchen table. "Cheer up: remember, you could have been born hideously deformed."

I wrote him five-page letters when he was gone. He wrote brief business notes back, mostly about the house, and love letters to Tucky. "What's going on here?" she asked. "Is he trying to make me into you or what?"

"Under no circumstances should your children be told," Paul's shrink had told him. "They're hardly children at twenty-three and twenty-six," my shrink told me. I insisted that Paul tell Tucky and Sam the truth or else I would.

"I want to be straight about what happened," I'd said. "I don't want any fake scenarios about women's lib."

"You want revenge," he said.

"Having gotten hold of the truth, I don't want to fudge it," I said.

"Oh, come on, civilized people know the virtues of concealment, they don't run around baring the truth."

In the end, he took each child to lunch separately in New York and told them he was a pederast and I an adulteress. For a civilized person, it was a brutal way of putting it. Sam cried. Tucky took it on the chin, and exploded later.

About a month after his return in December, Paul telephoned and asked me over formally, for cocktails. Friends had already told me that we were going to be reconciled. Paul had told them so. His lawyer had told my lawyer so. I was nervous and stiff when he answered the door. He gave me an embarrassed kiss, then sat me on our old sofa with the costly upholstery our cats had loved, poured me a glass of plonk, and set it on the custom-built Parsons coffee table we'd had tortoised, at considerable expense. His one new fixture, which seemed to cover the wall, was an antique American flag displaying an undulating snake: "Don't Tread on Me."

Paul sat opposite me on a chair and ticked off items on a list he held in his hand. One, a tax bill of $1,309.40, due February 1, must be paid on time or the borough would charge interest. Two, living alone in England, he'd found out how much he loved me and how much he hated living alone. Even if we got divorced, he wondered if we might not live together. Three, he'd discovered he was not homosexual. He didn't want to touch young boys, he just wanted to look at them. Four, he'd done what he'd done to punish me, because I didn't like his students, because I was jealous of them. It could have been a girl just as easily.

"But it wasn't," I said.

"Yeah, I *am* going to look for a therapist," he said.

And then he talked about his research in England, the university that was courting him, his new book, his new publisher, his latest magazine piece, his batches of fan mail from the last magazine piece. As I was halfway out the door, he said, "I must ask you sometime how your cookbook is going."

"Yes," I said. "That would be nice."

That he hadn't asked about anything made it easier to say goodbye to the house and the yard and the trees, along with the husband. A year allowed for a long goodbye, and I made the most of it, recording with pen and camera, as in a Book of Days, the seasonal changes inside and out. During the long, tenuous summer, I'd given up on my swamp garden. It was supposed to grow herbs, but the clay was so thick, the ground so wet, the shade so dark that only watercress and slugs had flourished. I set out pans of Budweiser to drown them in or, when I lost patience, ran out with a box of Morton's to salt them one by one until they shriveled and fell from leaf to ground as blobs of slime. I found I liked slug murder.

In the fall, the remaining elms, the tulip tree in front, the maples in back, the dogwoods at the side, the Japanese maple in the rock garden, the young hawthorn given us by a friend for our thirtieth anniversary, had exploded in squibs of red and orange and gold as if they knew this was a final burst. In winter snow lay like a goose-down comforter on the same garden and trees, turning the place into the frosting-roofed gingerbread house I had made one Christmas. I'd glued walls and roof together with stiff caramel and then, in a moment of hubris, set a candle inside so that light would glow through the little mullioned windows, forgetting that heat melts caramel until I saw the house softly implode, putting out the light.

In spring I'd numbered each star crocus, miniature daffodil, hyacinth, and narcissus as their green tips broke through the thawing earth. I knew when the purple clematis, when the white, would suddenly curtain the terrace with blossoms. I could clock the spring by when the tight rolls of pink on the vines covering the arbor relaxed into greening grape leaves. The salmon azaleas always blossomed before the white ones, as the white dogwood always emerged before the pink. The mountain laurel and the rhododendrons, twice replaced after killing frosts, were always last, as if they knew they capped the show.

These were the changes that soothed, because they were changeless. The changes inside the house were less predictable. For the first time ever I was living in a place where, if you discounted the cats, I was the sole occupant. I had dreaded the thought of living alone because I feared, like Paul, that I'd be lonely. Instead, I found I relished my new privacy. As soon as he was gone, I moved my work into his study. Like Goldilocks, I put my typewriter on his big desk, sat in his big chair, put my feet on his footstool, and spread out my growing manuscripts on his library table. I discovered that the Rhode Island maple four-poster we'd bought as a standard double, a margin of which I'd occupied while Paul sprawled, was a mere three-quarter bed. No wonder we were crowded. Now that it was all mine, I filled it with arms and legs spread from end to end and side to side like Leonardo da Vinci's drawing of proportionate man, the measure of all things.

I could read all night long if I wanted to, without the light disturbing anybody. I could talk on the bedside phone day or night for as long as I wanted, without fear of annoying anybody. I could eat anything I wanted, without having to prepare something different for someone else, and I could eat anytime I wanted to. I could go into New York without asking permission. I could buy food and clothing without asking for money. I could do cartwheels on the lawn, I could belt out Broadway show tunes without anybody's eyes rolling in disgust.

Before I left the house for good, I gave a smashing farewell brunch for seventy-five to honor and cleanse it. I cooked for a couple of weeks, old style, stretching the expandable table to the max with corn breads, creamed haddock, broiled kippers, sausage patties, crisp bacon, herbed frittatas, Austrian coffee cakes, smoked salmon, toasted bialys, and fresh pineapple with strawberries and mint from the herb garden, washed down with champagne and orange juice. The sun was out and the air was clear, as we spilled over the terrace and onto the lawn and under the trees on blankets and chairs. My last *petit déjeuner sur l'herbe*. I would never again have the same accumulation of friends in this spot that echoed with all our other parties. And

this time, if I got tired of doing the dishes, I could just throw
them like Frisbees across the lawn.

I knew just what to do with my new continent of freedom. I
wrote. I'd begun rewriting *Mabel* for the second time, from
scratch, in a rented studio—a room, really—in what had once
been the old Fifth Avenue Hotel on the corner of Ninth Street.
I'd done a thorough scholarly job of it the first time, but I
wanted to write a story for another kind of reader, another
kind of person, a person like me. I put a battered desk by the
window so that I could look out at the twin towers of the
World Trade Center, their beveled edges catching the light as
the sun moved east to west, marking time.

At noon I would stop typing and fetch from the half-fridge
tucked into the kitchen closet three slices of garlic salami, five
thyme-scented green olives, six cherry tomatoes or sometimes
the same number of cucumber slices, well salted. It was a ritual
consummation. I would remove the skin from each slice of
salami, eat a bite of meat and then an olive, removing the pit,
then put a cherry tomato in my mouth whole. The trick was to
make things come out even and last long, as if one were eating
a three-course meal. The quality was high since my local grocer
was Balducci's, and I had savored each food as perfect of its
kind, just as I savored the room, with its desk and bed and window, looking down into the seedy back rooms of Eighth Street
in the foreground and up at the inhuman rectangles of The City
at the horizon. I was eating New York.

I'd discovered that the ritual of eating was like the ritual of
writing. I wanted to clear my mind of junk, the way I'd cleaned
the house and emptied the fridge. I wanted to get down to bare
bones, elemental flavors, each word tasted in itself and in com-

bination with other words, what Yeats called the "right mastery of natural things." I wanted to eat my words, throw caution and footnotes to the winds, away with *ibid*.s and *op. cit*.s. I wanted to write the way people I liked to talk to talked, a slumgullion of American slang and Anglo-Saxon meat and Latin potatoes. My mentors in this new discipline were newspaper editors, as exacting in their way as my Harvard professors had been. I had to cast off what I'd learned and begin again if I were to write articles of no more than seven hundred and fifty words. I discovered that you could write the history of the world in five hundred, fifty, or five words if you had to. Even two would do: Adam wept.

I wrote in a kind of stubborn frenzy, hanging myself up on sentences that didn't go together, mired in words thick as pudding because I didn't know where I was going or where I'd come from. Given to metaphor more than logic, I sometimes feared there was something wrong with my brain that made the simplest declarative sentence as tricky as a soufflé. My head would dump a garbage bag of ideas in my lap and it would take me forever to select two or three choice bits to make a meal.

Meanwhile, I lurched from sublet to sublet, looking for a permanent home. I was determined to live in the Village, which I loved for its scale, its village feel. The Village, in fact, was the village I had always wanted when I lived in the suburbs and a loaf of bread meant a ten-minute drive and a twenty-minute hunt for a parking space. But in the city, you could walk down the street and greet by name the vegetable seller, the drugstore lady, the newspaper man, the bagel vendor, the shoe repair couple. They were like the villagers of Provence, only here they came in as many colors and kinds as the goods they sold.

After several months, I lucked into the attic of a Greek Revival Presbyterian church that, behind the six white Doric pillars of its facade, had been converted into apartments for people like me. The contractor had punctured the church roof with skylights because that was cheaper than punching more windows into the two-foot-thick walls. It was like living in California. Every room was awash in light, and the foot-thick oak beams and massive iron bolts that held up the roof hymned Christ the Nail from wall to wall. To think that I'd traveled three thousand miles and fifty-three years from my birthplace to end up in a Presbyterian church. When I lay in bed and looked up, there was nothing between me and eternity but the pigeons, airplanes, and God.

An odd thing was happening to my body. I had begun to take on flesh. I had weighed the same, had had roughly the same bony shape, except for pregnancies, since the day we married. Now, unaccountably, my breasts began to grow. This late middle-aged blooming was as unexpected as my first pubescent buds, and it made more than my clothes fit differently. By God, I really was a woman, not a failed man, and there were lots of men out there who liked women because they were different from men. For the first time in my life, I think, I began to like being what I was—a woman.

I flew to California and drove with my brother Bob to Rivino Orchards to see what was left of our memories. It was the first time either of us had returned to that spot. We drove through a rural slum, where cement dust sifted thickly onto rows of bungalows with sagging screen porches and rusting car skeletons under scaling eucalyptus trees. The cement plant had nearly consumed the hill behind it, evacuating it in little concrete turds.

Bob pointed out the intersection where Dad had smashed the wooden wheel of his Model T when he crashed broadside into another car. He found the field near our garage where a bull had once chased us, although there was no sign of the garage. But that wasn't the main reason we'd come. We wanted to visit Dad at the old-age home at the end of Brockton Avenue away from town, near the house where we'd once lived with our grandparents. Dad had been at the Center for fifteen years, so he'd occupied a number of rooms, but we found his present one, finally, at the end of a hall. Inside were three beds in a row. In the first, a woman lay under the covers howling. In the next, a man sat naked, his feet on the floor, his hands holding so tight to the edge of the bed that his knuckles were white. He didn't make a sound. In the third bed, Dad lay propped up by pillows. His eyes were closed, the lids gummed shut, their edges red and oozing. His hands on the coverlet were claws of bone. He was ninety then.

I touched his shoulder and whispered, "Daddy, it's Betty, Betty and Bob." Slowly he unglued his eyes a crack, but he did not see me. His eyes were clouded gray as cement and hazy as smog. Was he seeing spring lupine and Indian paintbrush on the Mohave? I held his hand. "Daddy." He worked his mouth a little, a long slit red as his eyes. A male nurse entered briskly and put some clothes in a closet. I asked if Meryl Harper was one of his patients. He was. "Is he awake, do you think? Is he always like this?" The nurse wasn't sure because he'd been on duty for only a couple of weeks, but he thought that, yes, he was usually like this. The woman had not once stopped howling.

"Let's get out of here," Bob said. He dropped me off at the corner of Emerson Street three blocks away, where the D.O. lived, and drove on to a parking lot by the drugstore, where he would wait for me.

"Well, blow me down, well, I never," the D.O. said when

she opened the door and saw me there. She was wearing her upper plate but missing her lower one. I hadn't seen her for three or four years, and she was more stooped now, in her printed terry-cloth robe with a sleeveless sweater over it. Her eyes were sharp and her frown focused as she scuttled to a card table set up in the kitchen, covered with boxes, folders, and papers. "Here you are," she said, "here's *Betty* right here and here's *Bob*." Next to our folders was one labeled *Funeral Expenses* and another, the thickest one, *To Do*. She was still shuffling through the files, muttering about how much she had to do, how she was going to take me through everything, the birthday cards, the bills, her Bible, her devotions in *Daily Bread*, a copy of the letter she meant to send me weeks ago, the troubles with her abdomen, back, eyes, ears, how her niece never came to take care of her, when I left to find Bob.

"We need a drink," we said in unison.

Dad died the next year, even though nobody in my family dies. He passed away from "heart stoppage" at ninety-one. Bob telephoned to tell me, and afterward I telephoned the D.O. "Hello, hello? I can't hear too good," she said. "I've lost my new hearing aid, not as young as I once was and I can't get everything done the way I'd like to, but I've got you on my list and I intend to sit right down and write, I've got so much to say, I had my notes right here somewhere . . ." I put the telephone back in its cradle. She hadn't once mentioned Dad.

Bob called again to tell me how the service went. Several members of the Cactus and Succulent Society had driven up from Joshua Tree National Monument, and the minister had made only a few mistakes. He called Dad a physicist and pronounced Meryl as two syllables instead of one. I was surprised that Dad had decided to be cremated rather than buried in the earth, as my mother had been, in Forest Lawn Cemetery outside Hollywood. When I was researching *Mabel*, I'd once located the small flat plaque that identified Hazel Kennedy Harper among the rolling green acres of plaques watched over by statues of Jesus. Several years after Dad's death, I visited the mortuary drawer in Riverside's Evergreen Cemetery that contained his ashes. It was the same cemetery where he'd buried his parents and taught me to drive. Later still, after the D.O.'s niece had moved her to a nursing home in Alhambra, she reported that Dad's ashes were gone. "What happened to them?" I asked. "Nobody knows," she said. "They've simply disappeared."

I knew I wouldn't have to journey back to Riverside ever again. Home is where the hearth is, and I had already lit new fires in my new stove. Things I'd lugged with me were a comfort, like Grandma H.'s wicker sewing basket with her thimble and a few odd teeth I'd saved. I put her egg slicer in a drawer and my dad's squeezer in a cupboard and lined the walls with books and rebuilt my little universe, implement by implement, in the kitchen.

The kitchen is the one place in which we're all required to begin again, each day, at ground zero—reborn after the death of sleep to feed the gut, brain, and soul by daily murder and redemption. Cooking and eating, as Lévi-Strauss has said, are a form of mediation between heaven and earth, life and death, in the workplace of the kitchen. The kitchen mediates between power and submission and love and hate and all the other dynamics of living and dying, day by day. It's the place where, if we but have eyes to see, we can see the miraculous in the ordinary—can see each day water turn into wine, wine into vinegar, flour into bread, milk into butter, butter into cheese, loaves and fishes into food for multitudes. In the kitchen, the literal and symbolic, visible and intelligible, are as indistinguishable as the body and blood of Christ in bread and wine, as the feathers of Quetzalcoatl in a dish of ground corn, or the smile of Buddha in a bowl of burning yak butter.

In the beginning was the mouth, like Eve's mouth, biting. "The beauty of the world is the mouth of a labyrinth," and at the center, "there God is waiting to eat him," Simone Weil once wrote of man the maze-walker. "Later he will go out again, but he will be changed, he will have become different, after being eaten or digested by God." Sam at six had put it more simply: "We're all inside God's stomach."

A friend of mine traveling in the southern Oriente of Ecuador wanted to try the black root that the shamans of the Shuar eat for the trance state that transports them to the Other Side. Being an American, my friend insisted on going it alone. After a day of violent vomiting, the hallucinations began at night. He found himself in a black tunnel, drawn inexorably toward the end, and as he drew close he saw that the end was the fanged open mouth and throat of a giant serpent, black tongue flickering. His terror was so great that he fought with all his might against entering that mouth, fought so hard that he broke the trance and shook with chills and fever. When he told a shaman what had happened, the shaman said, "You should have let me go with you. Then you would have let the serpent swallow you. That's what the journey is for."

To eat and be eaten is a consummation devoutly to be wished in a universe that is all mouth, where black holes have a prodigious appetite for stars and neutrinos are always changing flavors. Small wonder then that humans have but the one orifice for food, speech, and love, or that the mouth, in eating, speaking, kissing, should be the portal to the serpentine tubing of the gut, the electrical wiring of the brain, the palpitations of the heart. The mouth is the shaman's portal to the Other Side, whether the Other is a kosher-keeping Yahweh, a vegetarian Puritan, or a dieter's Thin Man. All foods, all mouths, are sacred to the force that created them, whatever sumptuary laws man invents to triumph over his enemies in the vain attempt to deny that all alike are food for the mouths of worms.

I began as a mouth, sucking mother's milk like gin, and will likely end as a mouth, as my father did, sucking Jell-O and Kool-Aid through a straw. On the back of my hands I see Grandma H.'s veins like blue earthworms tunneled just beneath the skin. On my face I see Grandma K.'s wrinkles. Without lines no life, without breakage no change, without being swallowed no swallowing. Once I stole from the seat of an airplane a sign that read: OCCUPIED BY A THROUGH PASSENGER. Not the end of the journey but the journey itself is the destination that keeps body and soul going. Shapes change, the form remains. The recipe is Ovid's.

Memories fail, as recipes do, because what's inside the head and what's on the plate are never the same, no matter how hungry we are to bring them together. The recipe for my grandma's instant applesauce would have to include her thumb on the knife and the pocket in the apron on her lap. And there is no recipe for my stockpot of memories which is always at the simmer and which I stir with that rescued wooden spoon, fishing out a chicken bone here, an onion skin there, sloughing off the gray scum that bubbles to the top, straining the liquid and hoping the broth is strong enough, clear enough, flavorful enough to make good soup. We're all cooking, as Allen Ginsberg said, in "the alphabet soup of time." And that soup, like the kitchen itself, cheats time, denying memory at the same time it evokes it in a hard-boiled egg, a scraped apple, the smell of an orange.

My round dining table is a kitchen midden of unpaid bills, half-spent candles, soiled napkins, mail-order catalogues I will never order from, tear sheets of recipes I will never make, last year's letters I will never answer. To eat I must push all this aside to make a breathing space for my plate and glass. But that's as it should be. I don't require linen, napery, crystal glasses, polished silver, or an altar with a priest to raise the wafer and the wine. I'll grant it's better when you break bread and lift a glass and share words as well as tastes with other people in tidy and civilized surroundings, but eating alone has its virtues and rewards. I'm in a sure Place now. I can smack my lips and groan out loud with pleasure, put a slice of bread to my nose and inhale deeply, lick my plate clean with my tongue without embarrassment. I can rejoice in the lamb, and the pork, and the beef without recrimination. I can eat my father slowly in a bowl of mashed potatoes, I can dilute the vinegar of my stepmother with the blessing of oil. I can give mouth-to-mouth resuscitation to a two-pound lobster drowning in a lake of butter as if each breath were a lover's kiss. And if I want to, I can write about it, in the deep communion of words.